CREW

W9-AWO-374

CREW
THE ROWER'S HANDBOOK

M. B. ROBERTS
PHOTOGRAPHS BY RONALD C. MODRA

STERLING

New York / London
www.sterlingpublishing.com

STERLING and the distinctive Sterling logo are registered
trademarks of Sterling Publishing Co., Inc.

Library of Congress Cataloging-in-Publication Data

Roberts, M. B. (Mary Beth)
    Crew : the rower's handbook / M.B. Roberts ; photographs by
Ronald C. Modra.
        p. cm.
    Includes bibliographical references.
    ISBN-13: 978-1-4027-4131-9
    ISBN-10: 1-4027-4131-6
    1. Rowing—Handbooks, manuals, etc. I. Title.

GV791.R63 2007
797.12'3—dc22

                                                    2007016988

        10   9   8   7   6   5   4   3   2   1

Published by Sterling Publishing Co., Inc.
387 Park Avenue South, New York, NY 10016
Photos © 2007 by Ronald C. Modra
Text © 2007 by M. B. Roberts
Distributed in Canada by Sterling Publishing
c/o Canadian Manda Group, 165 Dufferin Street
Toronto, Ontario, Canada M6K 3H6
Distributed in the United Kingdom by GMC Distribution Services
Castle Place, 166 High Street, Lewes, East Sussex, England BN7 1XU
Distributed in Australia by Capricorn Link (Australia) Pty. Ltd.
P.O. Box 704, Windsor, NSW 2756, Australia

Book design and layout by Amy Henderson
Photography by Ronald C. Modra

Printed in China
All rights reserved

Sterling ISBN-13:978-1-4027-4131-9
ISBN-10:1-4027-4131-6

For information about custom editions, special sales, premium
and corporate purchases, please contact Sterling Special Sales
Department at 800-805-5489 or specialsales@sterlingpub.com.

CONTENTS

AUTHOR'S NOTE

Rowing rules, regulations, and traditions in the United States often vary from region to region and between levels of competition. For simplicity's sake, this book cites the rules of USRowing, which the majority of scholastic, collegiate, and club crews also follow. Throughout the book, USRowing Rules are quoted with permission; rules referenced verbatim are shown italicized. Most of the terms in the "Coming to Terms" sections come from USRowing Rules and publications.

With this book, it is our goal to show aspiring rowers how to get involved in crew and to give them basic information. Individual rowers should also seek out information specific to their regions (especially about water conditions and safety), as well as local rules and regulations.

FOREWORD

The tradition of rowing dates back to the first intercollegiate sporting competition in the United States, and rowing at the highest level dates to the first modern Olympic Games. With this history, the sport of rowing is often misconceived as an elitist activity, pursued mainly in the Northeast at Ivy League colleges and at prep schools. While the Olympic tradition of our sport remains strong, the reality is that rowing has significantly changed during the past two decades. Many factors have caused a groundswell of participation among all ages in rowing, but none has had such a direct effect as the inclusion of women's rowing as an NCAA sport. Title IX provided the opportunity for large and small institutions to either add the sport outright or assimilate and elevate an existing club program to varsity status.

The inclusion of women's rowing has produced a ripple effect throughout the sport. As more nationally ranked athletic programs at colleges and universities created teams, their alumni became more familiar with the sport; high school programs blossomed in reaction to scholarship opportunities; and an older generation of parents and relatives became versed in the new sport, some becoming officials, volunteers, and often masters rowers themselves.

What has been the actual impact? In 1987, nearly four hundred programs representing thirty thousand individuals competed in the sport in the United States. Today, there are more than one thousand registered organizations, representing close to eighty thousand competitors. The growth is among all ages, and junior, collegiate, and masters.

Consequently, rowing is becoming more mainstream and accessible, with most rowing programs providing basic learn-to-row instruction and programs open to the novice. All that is needed to enjoy rowing is an enthusiasm to learn a new sport and a base level of athleticism.

As the national governing body for the sport, USRowing is the primary resource for interested participants to discover rowing: its clearinghouse offers information and knowledge on many topics. Athletes seeking to explore their opportunities in rowing also can access a directory of clubs and programs, as well as articles and educational materials. To promote the continued growth of the sport, USRowing constantly seeks volunteers to train as officials and coaches, the support structure for competition.

Rowing is a lifelong endeavor. Its focal points are teamwork, dedication, and determination. Each of these characteristics is basic to success in life, so it is no wonder that many leaders credit their time as oarsmen for their achievements later in life. Perhaps the best aspect of the sport is that anyone may join in at any time during his or her life, young or old. Rowing is a low-impact sport that can be enjoyed from a single-person scull to the team social eight-person shell. Local clubs are found throughout the United States and provide opportunities at all levels.

In the words of rowers everywhere: "Ready All, Row!"

Glenn Merry
USRowing Executive Director

Acknowledgments

Many thanks to Glen Merry at USRowing for his insights and ideas, as well as the use of USRowing Rules and other resources, and to Hart Perry at the National Rowing Foundation for his generosity in sharing historical records, photographs, and valuable contacts.

We would also like to acknowledge Paul O'Pecko for his assistance with research at the G.W. Blunt White Library at the Mystic Seaport and his permission to use materials resulting from that research.

Special thanks to the coaches, students, and alumni at the M.I.T. boathouse for their warm welcome and guided tour of the Charles. Thanks to Aaron Benson for contributing detailed information about training for this book.

Also, we would especially like to acknowledge Jaryn Finch, JV Coach, and Joel Skaliotis, Head Coach, at Brookline High School in Massachusetts, for lending us their crews and welcoming us into the Riverside Boathouse.

1: READY ALL?

What to Know If You Want to Row

So, you want to row? The first thing to know is some simple terminology: *Crew* refers to the group of rowers assembled to propel a racing boat through the water using oars. The rowers *row* (they don't *crew*), and the crew is just a crew (not a *crew team*). It's okay to say *rowing team* if you're talking about the whole shebang—the coach, the coxswain, the boatman, and the crew, but a crew is just a crew.

To go one step further, remember that the use of oarlocks or pins to hold the oars while rowing is what separates rowing from paddling. Rowers don't *paddle*, they *row*.

That's the easy part.

For those who want to learn about rowing and, possibly, to get involved in this elegant sport, there are a few slightly more difficult intellectual hurdles to clear. First, an oarsman faces backward to go forward. The smallest person on the crew appears to be in charge. Also, when someone from another crew gives you the shirt off his back, he isn't just being nice. It means your crew beat him in a race and he is honoring tradition by handing over his shirt. (And, yes, it is sweaty.)

In crew, *feathering* has nothing to do with a bird, and *catching a crab* is a bad thing. When rowers *catch and release*, it has nothing to do with fishing. When they *sweep*, there is no kitchen floor involved. And, in perhaps the most interesting paradox of all, rowing is called both the most accessible of sports (meaning a beginner can learn it fairly quickly) and the most challenging of sports (meaning the training and races are absolutely grueling).

Plus, there are cold morning practices, blisters, and pain to consider.

Still want to row?

The water awaits.

Miami nice: A crew has the water and the Miami skyline all to itself.

THE BIG PICTURE

It makes perfect sense that rowing is most popular and widespread in areas on or near the water. Lakes, reservoirs, or rivers with mellow currents are the most conducive to the sport and are often well traveled by recreational rowers, primarily scullers out for exercise.

NOTE: Ocean rowing, the more extreme arm of the sport, exists but is much more obscure due to the danger of rowing in waves.

Crews are most likely to be found in cities and towns where there is a history of rowing, such as Boston/Cambridge and Philadelphia. While the Northeast and Mid-Atlantic are traditionally considered the centers of rowing, there is also a long tradition in places such as San Diego, California, Washington State, and Wisconsin.

Recently, crew has been expanding to areas new to rowing, such as Florida (especially the Tampa area), Arizona, and many parts of the South, including Tennessee, Georgia, North Carolina, and Texas. These burgeoning bastions of crew have the weather advantage: it's warm most of the year, whereas except for annual spring break rowing trips to southern cities, northern crews are forced off the water and indoors to train in the winter.

These days, both girls and boys row in high school, and both men and women row in college and beyond. USRowing calls crew a great "walk-on sport," meaning many rowers try the sport for the first time—and learn it fairly quickly—at a later age than participants in other sports. It would be unusual to see a college freshman walk onto a baseball field and try out for the team if he had never swung a bat before. But rowing is different.

Crews in clubs, high school, and, for the most part, college are arranged by ability. High school and club crews almost always seat a

A coxswain takes command of her crew.

No pain, no gain.

novice boat where participants with less than one year of experience may learn to row and compete. Similarly, men's collegiate crews seat freshman boats as well as varsity (and a second or junior varsity, depending on the number of participants). Since women's rowing, unlike men's crew, is governed by NCAA rules that don't allow a provision for separate freshman teams, there are no separate squads for freshman women. Instead, most colleges field a women's novice crew so that less-experienced rowers will have a chance to practice and compete.

"Always remember, there's more to life than rowing—but not much."
—DONALD BEER, YALE CLASS OF '56

ARE GOOD ROWERS BORN OR MADE?

Both. There is definitely a body type for rowers. The best oarsmen tend to be tall and long-limbed with broad shoulders and strong legs. Most people mistakenly think the strength of a rowing stroke comes from the upper body; in fact, it comes from the legs. But rowing is a total body workout, fully utilizing all the parts. Anyone who is willing to work hard, show up for practice, and get in good cardiovascular shape can become an excellent rower.

Attitude and desire may be the most important factors in succeeding as an oarsman. We see this in the growth of adaptive rowing programs, where people with disabilities are given the opportunity to row. USRowing even seats a National Adaptive team that competes in the World Rowing Championships.

So Why Row?

Besides the fact that rowing is fantastic exercise, burning more calories than almost any other workout, many people are drawn to crew because it is the ultimate team sport. Besides single sculls, where just one rower moves the boat along the water, rowing is entirely about teamwork. Each member of the crew is vital, and no one oarsman is more important than any other. Hart Perry, executive director of the National Rowing Foundation and former coach at the Kent School in Connecticut, tells a story of a boy he once coached. "He had no chance of making the varsity," says Perry, "but he came to practice every day so that if someone didn't show up, the crew could still row. That was good for the crew and good for him."

When a crew is really working as a team, when they are in sync (also called "in swing") on the water, that's the payoff. Rowers say there's no feeling quite like a crew in swing and moving along the water in an effortless glide.

There is another payoff, too: the more a crew is in sync, the more successful it will be on race day. Rowers will always have different degrees of skill— some will always be better than others. But in crew, if one person tries to stand out, he will actually make the boat slower. When individuals work together and match their talent as well as their bladework, they will become a winning crew.

DOS AND DON'TS

Do say: Princeton has an awesome crew.
Don't say: Princeton has an awesome crew team.

Do say: They row really well.
Don't say: They crew really well.

Do ask: Is that your oar?
Don't ask: Is that your paddle?

THE BASICS

Rowing is divided into two distinct disciplines: *sweep rowing* and *sculling*.

- In sweep rowing, athletes hold one oar with both hands and row continually on one side.
- In sculling, they hold two oars, or sculls, one in each hand, and row on both sides simultaneously.

THE BOATS

Whether sweeping or sculling, there are six basic configurations of boats. Sweep rowers come in pairs (2s), fours (4s), and eights (8s), also

A sculler glides down the Charles River.

"Rowing at its best is the symmetry of powerful athletes pulling on their oars at precisely the right moment."—DAVID HALBERSTAM, *THE AMATEURS*

Hearts begin to race as a crew approaches the water.

known as "the big boats," which are what many people think of when they hear the word "crew." Scullers row in singles (1×), doubles (2×), and quads (4×). Bigger boats do exist (for example, the 24 Stampfli Express or an eight-person scull called an *octet*), but they are extremely rare.

All eights carry a *coxswain* (pronounced "cox-n"), the person who steers the boat and serves as the on-the-water coach. Sweep rowers (pairs and fours) and sculls (doubles and quads) may or may not have one on board, but coxes on sculls are relatively rare.

In sweep boats without coxswains, one rower steers the boat by using a rudder controlled with his foot. In sculls without coxswains, the rowers steer mostly by increasing or decreasing the pressure on one oar scull or the other, as sculls are not equipped with a rudder. Since most high-school and collegiate crews row sweep, that's what we will emphasize here.

CATEGORIES

Rowers, and thereby the races they compete in, are categorized by sex, age, and weight. (USRowing further categorizes by skill, as in elite, senior, and intermediate.) Competitions are offered for men and women, and (on rare occasions. usually masters events) for mixed crews. Junior events are organized for rowers 18 or under who spent the previous year in high school.

NOTE: Individual schools that sponsor their own crews are called *scholastic programs*, whereas club crews drawing from many high schools in an area are referred to as *youth* or *junior programs*.

Masters events are held for rowers 27 and older. Collegiate events are divided into novice for women, freshman for men, and varsity (broken down to second or junior varsity depending on number of boats) for both.

USRowing defines two weight categories for both women and men: *open* and *lightweight*. Designations vary slightly in different leagues or regions. For example, most colleges refer to their men's nonlightweight crews as *heavyweight*, with weight minimums from 160 to 170 pounds (72.5 to 77 kilograms, kg). Weights in the USRowing National Team Trials regattas, and regattas governed by the International Rowing Federation (FISA), also vary. In any case, the weights always refer to the rowers, not the boats, and a boat average is also calculated.

According to USRowing Rules:

Open events are those that are not lightweight events.

Lightweight event crews are defined as follows:

A men's lightweight crew shall average no more than

WEIGH IN

Competitors, including coxswains, are weighed at events (once each day for multiday regattas), no earlier than two hours and no later than one hour before the starting time of their particular race. Athletes are weighed in their racing uniform, without shoes or other footgear.

155 lbs. [70.5 kg] per rower, and no individual rower shall weigh more than 160 lbs [72.5 kg]. The coxswain shall not be counted for purposes of this rule. A male single sculler (1×) shall not weigh more than 160 lbs [72.6 kg]. A junior men's lightweight crew is one in which no individual rower weighs more than 155 lbs [70.3 kg]. A men's masters lightweight crew is one in which no individual rower weighs more than 160 lbs [72.5 kg].

A women's lightweight crew, including a single scull (1×), shall have no rower who weighs more than 130 lbs [59 kg]. The coxswain shall not be counted for purposes of this rule.

NOTE: Lightweights row the same events as open-weight athletes. Lightweight eights carry a coxswain, but doubles and fours do not.

SEATING

Rowers are identified by the position or seat they maintain in the boat. In an eight boat, the *bow person* or *bow oar* sits in the bow (the front of the boat, most often the farthest position from the coxswain). This is also known as "number one" (as in the first person in the shell). The rower in front of the bow is number 2 (or the "2 seat"), then number 3, number 4, number 5, number 6, number 7, and number 8—the rower seated in front of the coxswain, who is also called the *stroke oar*. The "stroke" is always a strong rower with outstanding technique, a leader of the crew charged with setting the pace for the other athletes in the boat.

Sometimes the rowers are referred to not by their specific seats but by the section they occupy. In an eight (or a four), the bow oar and 2 seat are referred to as the *bow pair*, and the 7 seat and stroke (or the 3 seat and stroke in a four) are referred to as the *stroke* or *stern pair*.

Harvard men aim for swing.

Bow, 2, 3, and 4 seats are the *bow four* while stroke, 7, 6, and 5 are the *stern four*. The 3, 4, 5, and 6 seats (or the *middle four*) are nicknamed "the engine room" of the boat.

The odd-numbered seats row to the port side (the left side when facing forward) while the even-numbered seats row to the starboard side (the right side when facing forward).

If all this sounds complicated, it may be helpful to think of rowers' placement on the boat in terms of what they do.

Stroke. Often the most talented rower, the stroke sits facing the coxswain and sets the pace for the rest of the crew. Coaches say the stroke should be not only a strong athlete but the most precise and controlled oar as well.

7-seat. Along with the stroke, serves as one of two "lead dancers" on the boat. This pairing is critical to the rhythm of the boat.

THE BOUNDING MAIN

Although ocean rowing is a sport in its own right, it is a bit more obscure than the rowing practiced on more placid rivers and lakes. It is sort of the X-Games version of rowing, with the high adventure factor brought in by attempting to row on waves.

Despite the danger factor, several well-known ocean rowing events take place every year, including the Isles of Shoals race, from New Hampshire's Isle of Shoals to Portsmouth Harbor, and California's annual thirty-six-mile race from Catalina Island to Marina Del Rey.

Engine room. These are the tallest and heaviest rowers, seated in the middle and sturdiest part of the boat. They have demonstrated strength and excellent endurance and provide much of the boat's power.

Bow pair. These two seats, often occupied by the lightest rowers, are about finesse. They provide the balance and direction of the boat.

It's the coach's job to decide who sits where. It used to be that if an athlete learned to row port, he would always row port. But that is changing. Many high school or novice coaches today teach young oarsmen to row both sides from the beginning. This kind of flexibility definitely works in a rower's favor if he continues to row in college and beyond.

In seating the boat, the coach effectively balances the boat in terms of weight and strength. (He doesn't want his heaviest or strongest rowers all on one side, or the boat will never go straight!) Some corrections can be made for a slight imbalance when rigging the boat, but it's best to get the right people in the right (or left!) places from the start.

COMING TO TERMS

A coach shadows a shell in his launch.

Here's the what and the who, as defined by USRowing:

Competitor: Any person who participates in a crew as a rower or coxswain.

Coxswain: Any competitor in a crew who is not a rower and who, apart from operating a bona fide steering mechanism, does not participate in the physical propulsion of the boat.

Crew: An entity composed of competitors and constituted for the purpose of competing in an event at a regatta. A crew shall be considered an entity subject to these rules, and members of a crew shall be collectively responsible for its conduct, from the time it has launched until it has returned to land.

Novice: A coxswain or rower whose initial competition within that same discipline has been in the previous 12 months to the date of the regatta.

Rower: Any person acting as an oarsman or oarswoman who participates in the physical propulsion of a boat.

Rowing: The propulsion of a displacement boat through water by the muscular force of one or more rowers, with or without a coxswain, in which oars are levers of the second order, and in which the rowers are sitting with their backs to the direction of forward movement of the boat.

Scull: An oar used in a boat in which each rower uses two oars. "Scull" also shall refer to boats and events in which such oars are used.

Sweep: An oar used in a boat in which each rower uses one oar. "Sweep" also shall refer to boats and events in which such oars are used.

Team: Shall mean all competitors, coaches, managers, trainers, boatmen, and other administrators who represent the same club at a particular regatta. A team and members thereof shall be considered constituted and subject to these rules throughout a regatta.

2: FROM SLAVES TO FAST EIGHTS

The Story of Rowing

Most scholars, most historians, and certainly most rowers agree: rowing is the first modern sport. Born of necessity—early civilizations traveled, fished, traded, and frequently made war in boats that were centuries away from having motors—rowing eventually evolved into an activity that people did for fun, exercise, prestige, and sometimes prize money. But it took a while.

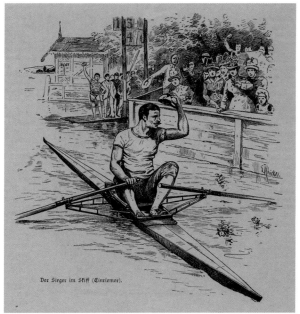

Der Sieger im Skiff (Einriemer).

Late eighteenth-century German lithograph. Courtesy of the National Rowing Foundation.

DAYS OF OAR

First, we need to go way back in time. Think Cleopatra being rowed down the Nile while a drumbeat keeps her oarsmen in time. Or picture Ben Hur and other slaves made to row in chains on Roman ships, until some of them literally drop dead. In fact, rowing got its name from this very scene: oarsmen packed tightly together in rows. (Today's college crews may find the bondage image involuntarily comes to mind during especially grueling morning practices.)

By 3000 BC, Phoenicians and Egyptians were using oars to move their enormous trading ships and barges along the coasts and rivers. The ancient Greeks built warships that were often propelled by more than two hundred oarsmen. According to Stephen Kiesling, the accomplished rower who wrote *The Shell Game*, history documents that the outnumbered Athenian navy consistently defeated the Persian fleet. One of the reasons? The Athenian oarsmen (as depicted in ancient pottery paintings) were evidently the first to row on sliding seats, using their legs, as well as their arms and backs, as modern crews do.

The ancient Romans, Carthaginians, Babylonians, Polynesians, and Venetians, as well as the Vikings, all had large rowing galleys in their fleets. For centuries, rowing was the most common form of power for river, lake, and sea travel; and even after the Phoenicians introduced sails to their boats, oarsmen continued to be a crucial element of ancient life. A huge technical improvement—the development of the oar working against a fulcrum—was introduced some time around 1000 BC and made rowing an even more efficient mode of transportation.

PLEASURE BOATS

The life of an ancient oarsman was far from idyllic, given the uncharted waters, rustic equipment, and often cruel treatment and conditions. Plus, early rowers had to contend with their share of ancient superstitions adopted by men of the sea. One was the belief that it was unlucky to cut your hair or nails at sea; these were offerings to Persephone, Goddess of the Underworld, and if they were offered on Poseidon's turf, the God of the Sea would get jealous and make for a rocky trip. Even so, it wasn't all work and no play for early "crews." History and literature contain a number of references to rowing for pleasure, the earliest in Homer's *Odyssey*, when Ulysses is greeted by boat-rowing islanders as he returns to Ithaca.

The crews on ancient Greek and Phoenician ships were usually slaves and criminals.

We also know that boats propelled by oarsmen were featured time and again in ceremonies and processions throughout the ancient world—a much better gig for a rower than an ocean voyage or a naval battle.

It's easy to imagine that from the earliest time, wherever two or more vessels were put into the water, impromptu races broke out. It is said that boat races were included in the Panathenaic and Isthmian games of ancient Greece (featuring fishermen and crews from the big galleys as competitors).

But the first documented example of rowing as an organized competitive sport again comes from literature. In Virgil's *Aeneid*, a piece of political propaganda commissioned by Augustus, Rome's first emperor, in the first century AD, a race is a focal point of the funeral games organized by Aeneas in honor of his deceased father, Anchises.

The first mention of a regatta, most likely a grand parade of boats, appears in Venetian documents around 1274. Venice, with its vast system of canals and waterways, was the ideal site for such events, and by 1315, boat races were featured prominently in the life of the city.

JOLLY OLD ENGLAND

As a sea-surrounded nation whose identity and empire would be built on the backs of ships, England was also an ideal locale for the evolution of rowing. British history is peppered with references to kings, queens, and other nobles being regally transported from town to town along its waterways.

In *The Book of Rowing*, D.C. Churbuck writes that Edgar the Peaceful was rowed down the River Dee in 1080 by provincial kings, with Edgar at the helm, acting as coxswain.

The most regal processions took place on the Thames, England's most fabled and important river, beginning in 1454 when the Lord Mayor of London, Sir John Norman, made his first pilgrimage from London to Westminster. The mayor's trip, made courtesy of watermen with silver oars rowing an elaborate barge, became an annual event that later expanded into a lively celebration featuring dozens of lavish barges and plenty of pomp and ceremony. The event continued for centuries, until 1856, and as noted in "A Brief Time-Line of Rowing" (compiled by the Friends of Rowing History and the National Rowing

Foundation), no doubt inspired generations of future rowers, especially those young Englishmen who attended the prestigious Eton College, the United Kingdom's foremost private school for boys, located on the Thames at Windsor.

But the River Thames was not just a corridor for ceremonial boating. It was, and is, an active, working waterway. According to *The Book of Rowing*, in the early 1700s, more than ten thousand Londoners earned their living on the Thames, the majority of them oarsmen aboard barges, lighters, and small boats known as cocks or gigs. All this hard work (as well as competition for jobs and for passengers who sought quick trips across the river) often led watermen to break into spontaneous races.

Then in 1715, a famous Irish actor named Thomas Doggett made the practice official when he organized a race on the Tideway in London and awarded a prize to winning watermen in their first year of apprenticeship. The Doggett Coat and Badge, the oldest continuously running athletic contest in the world, is still being run today, although contemporary races feature sleek sculls instead of bulky barges.

Rowing-related activities continued on the Thames throughout the eighteenth century. Although it's unclear when the first regatta was

VERY SUPERSTITIOUS

Many ancient rowers subscribed to superstitions adopted by sailors and other seagoing men. Some common myths:

■ Flowers were thought to be unlucky because they could be used as a funeral wreath if someone died on board.

■ Women, who were thought to anger the sea gods, were bad luck on boats. However, a naked woman, whose bare breasts were said to calm the sea, was thought to bring good luck—hence the tradition of vessels carrying a bare-breasted figure-head of a woman on the bow.

■ Pouring wine on the deck as an offering to the gods brought good luck.

■ Disaster was said to follow the oarsman who stepped onto a boat with his left foot first.

■ Anything black on board (luggage, clothing) was believed to bring bad luck because black is the color of death. The exception? A black cat, thought to be lucky at sea, even though unlucky on land.

held, the most significant early "water festival" took place at Ranelagh Gardens at Chelsea on the Thames in 1775. By all accounts this was a festive event during which oarsmen competed for prizes, and everyone from the humblest members of the working class to the royal family gathered along the river's banks to watch and cheer.

During this time, sporadic rowing competitions were also taking place in other parts of the world. For example, in the United States, there are records of two Philadelphia sporting clubs racing four- and six-oared barges on the Schuylkill River in 1762. Later, in 1811, two New York Whitehall fours, the Knickerbocker and the Invincible, raced from Harsimus, New Jersey, to Manhattan's Battery. There are also accounts of boat races in Australia, Russia, Canada, and other parts of Europe around the early 1800s.

Still, between the mid-1700s and the mid-1800s, the rowing headlines, such as they were, definitely belonged to the Brits. And many of the boldest headlines featured the word "Eton."

A major milestone: the first Oxford-Cambridge race was rowed in 1829.

In 1793, Eton hosted its first Procession of Boats, which began its long-honored custom of rowing competition among boys at the school. Although formal racing records weren't kept until 1817, it is well documented that Eton students raced in a ten-oared barge as well as several eight-oared boats in 1811, the same year that boating at their rival, London's Westminster School, evidently got under way.

Many Eton (and Westminster) students went on to study at Oxford and Cambridge, no doubt bringing their enthusiasm for competitive

Harvard crew in the tank, February 2, 1889.
Courtesy of the National Rowing Foundation.

rowing with them, since both Oxford (in 1815) and Cambridge (in 1827) had enough participants to organize their first boat clubs.

A major milestone in rowing history was marked in 1829 when the first Oxford-Cambridge race was rowed in eight-oared cutters before some twenty thousand onlookers at Henley-on-Thames. Oxford won. Rumors swirl to this day regarding the amount of betting on the first (and subsequent) races. (Some put the figure as high as 500 pounds.)

The 1-mile [1.6-km] and 550-yard [503-meter, m] race course, which is relatively straight and surrounded by gorgeous scenery, ultimately became the site of the Henley Royal Regatta, which was established in 1839 and remains *the* ultimate destination for competitive rowers, as well as a highlight of the British social season.

NOTE: The approximately mile and a quarter distance, also known as the "Henley distance," is unusual when compared to the international standard of two thousand meters, or the classic standard of four miles.

As rowing became more popular, improvements were continually sought to make boats lighter and faster. In 1828, Anthony Brown, of Newcastle-on-Tyne, developed the first outriggers, the triangular-shaped metal arms that extend from the side of the boat and support the oarlock and oar. These early riggers were placed at bow and stern and were used primarily to increase leverage. Then, in 1844, a racing single, equipped with outriggers as well as an inboard keel, made its appearance on the Thames. The first keel-less boats (with spoon-shaped oars), built by Henry Clasper of Oxford, followed in 1848.

Cornell crew (top) and Leander crew (bottom) at Henley, *Harper's Weekly,* **late 1800s.** Courtesy of the National Rowing Foundation.

Perhaps the most significant improvement—the sliding seat with wheels—was introduced sometime in the mid-1800s (more likely, reintroduced, since evidence from Greek artifacts suggests that ancient rowers used them). Most historians agree that Englishman Walter Brown first raced a sliding seat single in 1861; by 1870, many crew boats also featured sliding seats. Most rowers of the time surely found that these seats were an improvement on an earlier effort to achieve the same effect: greasing a stationary seat and sliding on top of it in leather trousers.

This major invention, which changed the way rowers moved the boat, because they could now use their legs for power, has been widely attributed to J. C. Babcock, the captain of the Nassau Boat Club in New York. Although others, including Germans and Englishmen, were working on different versions of moving seats with various materials, Babcock's version was most likely the first to work.

ACROSS THE POND

Babcock's success reminds us that although the British exerted vast influence on rowing equipment, coaching styles, techniques, and traditions in the nineteenth century, the Americans were making their own brand of rowing history.

According to "The Brief Time-Line of Rowing," in 1823 the New York-based Knickerbocker Club became the first boat club organized in the United States.

NOTE: *A Short History of American Rowing* lists the Detroit Boat Club, founded in 1839, as "the oldest club in the country still active in the sport."

New York was home to another historical event when it served as host to America's first international race between the Whitehall boat *American Star* and *Certain Death*, a boat manned by a crew from the British warship *Hussar*. The two four-oared boats raced four miles from the Battery flagstaff to Hoboken Point and back for an unheard-of $1,000 prize, offered by the captain of the *Hussar*. The New Yorkers won, much to the delight of the crowd of fifty thousand spectators, who had no doubt placed bets of their own.

In the spring of 1843, American collegiate rowing got its official start when a Yale student purchased a secondhand Whitehall boat for $29.50, brought it to New Haven, and, along with several other fellow undergrads, formed Yale's now legendary rowing club.

The next year, Harvard formed its own boat club in Cambridge, Massachusetts, starting what would become arguably the most storied collegiate crew (not to mention igniting the most intense rowing rivalry) of all time.

In 1852, Harvard's and Yale's crews climbed into their respective eights and raced each other over a three-mile course for the first time. Harvard won the race, which was organized by a local lodge and rowed on Lake Winnepesaukee, New Hampshire, on August 3. "The Race," as it would come to be known when it became a highly anticipated annual event, had the distinction of being the first intercollegiate athletic contest in the United States.

For the following decade or so, the Harvard-Yale race was rowed on different neutral courses, including the Connecticut River at Springfield, Lake Quinsigamond in Worcester, and Saratoga Springs in New York.

In 1878, the rival crews met for the first time on the Thames River in New London, Connecticut, where they still meet every June for an intense four-mile race that for decades was the undisputed social event of the season. Both Harvard and Yale put enormous stock in this event—so much so that each school maintains a boathouse along the Thames (Harvard's "Red Top" and Yale's "Gales Ferry"), which it occupies for only one month a year just prior to the race.

During the late nineteenth century, rowing was an extremely popular spectator sport worldwide; clubs were

Tank exercises, *The Illustrated American*, March 8, 1890. Courtesy of the National Rowing Foundation.

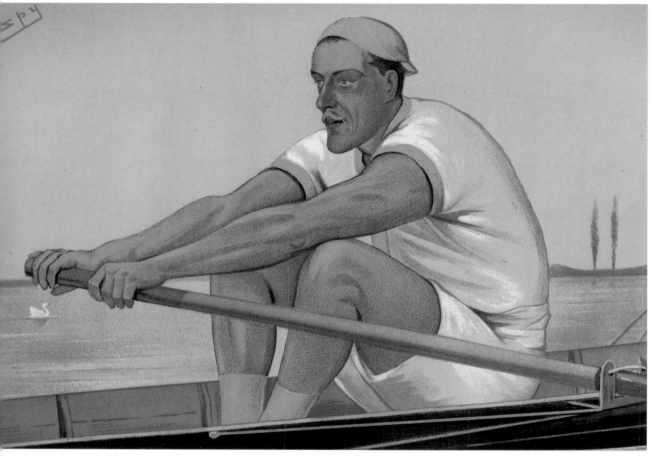

Vanity Fair **lithograph, March 22, 1890.** Courtesy of the National Rowing Foundation.

formed in Argentina, Peru, Denmark, France, Germany, Japan, Portugal, Canada, Mexico, South Africa, New Zealand, Australia, Russia, and Poland, to name just a few.

In 1869, Harvard traveled across the Atlantic to race Oxford on "the other Thames" in the first transatlantic amateur boat race. (Harvard lost.) More than half a million rowing fans gathered for the race, which was widely covered in the press, leading to even more interest in the already popular sport in the United States. It's difficult to fathom in this era of nightly ESPN highlights, but the *New York Times* splashed Columbia's victory in the 1874 collegiate rowing championships (attended by some twenty-five thousand spectators) across its entire front page.

Interest in rowing as a participant sport was definitely growing among prep school students (St. Paul's in Concord, New Hampshire, had an active club by 1870) and in colleges, especially those located near the rivers flowing through and around the East Coast cities of Philadelphia, New York, and Boston. Even women's colleges got into the act when, in 1875, Wellesley College established the oldest surviving organized women's rowing program. Charles Courtney, a rowing champion who later became a famous coach for Cornell, also began training women to row at Union Springs Seminary during this time. And in 1892, ZLAC, the first U.S. women's rowing club, was founded

Championship rowers—especially single scullers—were famous heroes, much like boxers would become in the 1900s.

in San Diego. (ZLAC is an acronym formed from the first letters of the first names of its founders: sisters Lena, Agnes, and Caroline Polhamus, and their best friend, Zulette Lamb. The club is still going strong.)

Harvard coach R.C. Lehmann, *Harper's Weekly*, late 1800s.
Courtesy of the National Rowing Foundation.

The number of regattas around the country, and the community rowing clubs that sponsored them, were also on the rise. According to *A Short History of American Rowing*, regattas increased in number from just a dozen before the Civil War to 150 in 1872, and were held in towns from Savannah to Sacramento and Mystic to Milwaukee.

FOR FUN AND PROFIT

College crew, 1800s. Courtesy of the National Rowing Foundation.

As much as rowing was growing as an amateur sport, there were even more opportunities for professionals in the late 1800s, an era that is often described as the Golden Age of Rowing.

THE PROS

It makes perfect sense that a man (women only rowed for pleasure or their health during these years) who was a talented, strong rower would rather make his living by racing on the water than unloading barges or ferrying passengers from ship to shore.

One such man was the famous Canadian oarsman Edward "Ned" Hanlan (a.k.a. "the Boy in Blue"), who broke out as an amateur by winning the singles championship at the U.S. Centennial celebration in Philadelphia. After turning pro in 1877, Hanlan won many more competitions, including the first professional rowing World Championship title in 1880, which he held until he was defeated by William Beach in 1884.

Professional rowing could be very lucrative both for the rowers themselves (purses often ranged from $25 to $6,000, and scullers often made up to $15,000 a year) and for the gamblers who followed the races. This temptation of riches actually proved the undoing of the

professional side of the sport around the start of the twentieth century. With such high stakes, dirty tricks and rigged races became the order of the day. For example, a highly anticipated rematch between rivals Charles Courtney and

California varsity crew. Courtesy of the National Rowing Foundation.

Ned Hanlan was canceled because someone sawed Courtney's boat in half the night before the race and he refused to row in another boat. Soon, fed-up fans and sponsors lost interest.

THE AMATEURS

Concern about the potential corruption in professional rowing had been growing for years. Back in 1872, the National Association of Amateur Oarsmen (NAAO) was formed in an attempt to keep the amateur side of competition separate from the shadier pro side. The NAAO, which a century later would become the United States Rowing Association—now USRowing—was the first national amateur team sport organization in the United States.

Although well intentioned, the attempt to dissociate from the pros probably contributed to the sport's decline in popularity, as many people perceived rowing with no chance of monetary rewards to be elitist. The expense of the sport and the prevalence of rowing programs at Ivy League universities and exclusive prep schools underscored this image, which was mirrored across the Atlantic.

Ever since England's most popular regattas went from featuring races between working oarsmen in the early 1700s to contests between the nonworking "gentlemen" of the upper crust in the mid-1800s, the perception of rowing had undergone a major shift.

In fact, the Brits took their definition of "amateur" to such an extreme that for years, anyone who had ever performed manual labor (among other restrictions) was excluded from competing at the Royal Henley. Perhaps the most infamous snub came in 1927 when Jack Kelly, the U.S. champion single sculler and owner of a Philadelphia brick company, was excluded from competing because he was a former brick-layer. Perhaps the royals might have been more permissive if they had known that Kelly was the future father of Grace Kelly, later known as Princess Grace of Monaco. (Kelly's son Jack Jr. later avenged his father when he was allowed to compete and won the Diamond Sculls at the Royal Henley in 1956.)

Although no oarsmen in the United States would be denied the opportunity to compete based on their work history, American rowing in

Saturday Evening Post,
August 15, 1936.
Courtesy of the National
Rowing Foundation.

the early 1900s was definitely a pursuit for amateurs. By the turn of the century, Eastern Ivy League schools still dominated the sport, but programs were popping up in the Midwest (in Wisconsin) and the West (at Stanford and the University of California) and produced successful crews.

And at the University of Washington, the program did more than just succeed. Coach Hiram Conibear, an athletic trainer who took over the rowing program for the Huskies in 1904, with no previous experience as an oarsman or coach, effectively changed rowing by inventing a new stroke: the Conibear. This incredibly fast and effective hybrid merged the English orthodox style of rowing with American conditions; it was adapted by many oarsmen nationwide, especially when former Washington rowers went on to coach at other schools. Washington State gained another note of rowing distinction when the Pocock family settled in Seattle in 1912 and went on to become famous boatbuilders, turning out nearly every shell rowed by an American crew from 1930 to 1970.

THE OLYMPIANS

The ultimate destination for a sport dominated by amateurs is the Olympics. When the first modern Olympiad got underway in Athens in 1896, rowing events were on the schedule, but they were canceled due to bad weather. Thus, rowing did not make its modern Olympic debut until the Paris games in 1900, when the American eight, a crew from Philadelphia's Vesper Boat Club, won the gold. The American crews dominated the next Olympics, at St. Louis in 1904, with Vesper again winning the gold.

The United States did not send boats to the 1908 or 1912 Olympic Games, and World War I interrupted boat racing from 1914 to 1918.

But, despite a decade-long setback, the Americans dominated international rowing for the next forty years. Crews from the United States, many of them collegiate champs who rowed together at Yale, the Naval Academy, Berkeley, and the University of Washington, won the eights in every Olympics from 1920 to 1956.

Today, Olympic crews are selected differently. Instead of fielding a championship college or club team as a unit, the Olympic committee holds extensive camps and tryouts to seat boats from a pool of the best oarsmen in the country.

Beginning in the 1960s, the most significant challenge Olympic-class rowers have faced is competition from international crews whose training and competition are completely subsidized by their governments. (From the 1960s through the 1980s, the Soviet bloc countries fielded incredibly successful crews under this system.) With no promise of financial gain or opportunity to make a living as a pro, it takes complete dedication to become a United States Olympic champion rower.

The gold-medal-winning eight in the 1924 Olympics hailed from Yale and featured oarsman (and future baby doctor and beloved author) Benjamin Spock.

HERE COME THE GIRLS

Rowing today is enjoying enormous growth, and much of it can be directly traced to 1972, when the passage of Title IX promised parity in women's sports.

Although women were rowing at Wellesley College as early as 1877, their participation was always seen as secondary to men's and also, rather

Rowing is the quintessential team sport.

condescendingly, good for their health. Then, incredible as it may seem today, there were several decades in the twentieth century when the consensus was that exercise was not good for women, especially those in their childbearing years. But in the 1960s, as part of the push for women's equality in all areas of life, a slow, steady movement began for more opportunities for women and girls to participate in sports.

The National Women's Rowing Association, founded in 1962, held its first Nationals in Seattle in 1966, with only 100 competitors. Then, post-Title IX, girls began competing in the Scholastic Rowing Association (formerly the Schoolboy Rowing Association of America) in 1974.

Today, American women row at almost every college that offers a men's program, and U.S. women are consistently at the top of the heap internationally. Gone are the days when women had to stage a nude protest to gain shower facilities or decent equipment, as some of the 1976 Yale women's crew (some of them fresh from the world championships) memorably did.

Another factor in the recent growth in rowing can be traced to improvements in equipment. With the development of "recreational" shells that are more stable and less expensive than traditional racing shells, more beginners are trying the sport.

Also, more people (young and old) than ever are looking for a way to exercise and stay fit. Rowing is one of the best forms of exercise there is—it's low-impact, almost anyone can do it (including many disabled people), and it is one of the most effective full-body workouts.

Off-water warm-up.

Further, more and more children and adults are taking the opportunity to row as the number of clubs nationwide continues to rise: USRowing counted five hundred clubs as part of its membership in 1994. At the time of writing, the number is more than eleven hundred. The most explosive growth has occurred in areas that have not traditionally featured scholastic or collegiate programs, such as the South and Southwest.

So, whether a potential rower is attracted to the sport because of its beauty and grace, because he or she wants to be part of a team, or because he or she wants to be challenged to the fullest, where there is water and a will, there is a way.

Traditionally, every crew carries its own shell to and from the water.

MILESTONES IN MODERN ROWING HISTORY

1715

Modern racing begins with the first Doggett Coat and Badge race, the oldest continuously running athletic contest in the world.

1793

Eton sponsors the first Procession of Boats.

1843

The first U.S. collegiate boat club is organized at Yale, in May. Harvard follows the next year.

1852

Harvard and Yale race for the first time, at Lake Winnepesaukee, New Hampshire, on August 3. In the first intercollegiate athletic contest in the United States, Harvard wins.

1868

A famous American expression is coined after a crimson-wearing crew from Harvard beats Yale, and a Worcester, Massachusetts, newspaper reports that "a crowd of jubilant supporters celebrated well into the night and 'painted the town red.'"

1869

Oxford defeats Harvard in coxed fours on the Thames before five hundred thousand spectators in the first transatlantic amateur boat race.

The Columbia crew, *Harper's Weekly*, June 22, 1878. Courtesy of the National Rowing Foundation.

1870

Yale crews integrate the legs into rowing. (Oarsmen wore greased leather trousers and slid up and back on smooth wooden plates mounted where the tracks of the slide are positioned today.)

1871

Modern rolling seats are introduced. (And it is assumed that Yale puts away its greased leather trousers.)

1873

Bob Cook, the Yale captain, learns the English style of stroking at Oxford and introduces it to American college rowing, where it becomes the dominant collegiate stroke for several decades.

1878

The annual Harvard-Yale Regatta moves to New London, Connecticut, where it has been raced every June since.

1895

The newly formed Intercollegiate Rowing Association (IRA) begins holding its four-mile championship races for eights on the Hudson River at Poughkeepsie, New York. The event moves to the Ohio River at Marietta, then to Lake Onondaga at Syracuse. Today it is held on the Cooper River at Camden, New Jersey.

1896

F.J. Furnivall, an avid oarsman and cofounder of the *Oxford English Dictionary*, establishes the Hammersmith Sculling Club for Girls and Men (today's Hammersmith Sculling Club), inspired by his belief that "the exclusion of women from aquatic sport was pernicious."

1896

Professional rowing events are eliminated from the Boston city regattas, signaling the end of pro competition in the United States.

1900

Rowing makes its modern Olympic debut in Paris, with an American eight taking the gold.

1916

Joe Wright introduces lightweight rowing to American colleges at the University of Pennsylvania.

1923

A western crew (the University of Washington) wins the IRAs for the first time.

1926

The Oxford University Women's Boat Club is formed.

1927

The Kent school becomes the first schoolboy crew to race at Henley.

1938

Ernestine Bayer, one of the most influential women in rowing, founds the Philadelphia Girls' Rowing Club (PGRC).

1939

The Dad Vail Rowing Championships, held on the Schuylkill River in Philadelphia, and named for pro sculler and Wisconsin coach Harry Emerson "Dad" Vail, are established to allow equitable competition for smaller collegiate programs.

1961

Cambridge trains for the Boat Race using an Australian device called an "ergometer."

1963

Harry Parker is hired as Harvard's head coach and leads his crew to an upset of Yale, the first of 18 consecutive wins in the Race. He becomes the most successful and respected U.S. college coach in history.

1964

The U.S. National Women's Rowing Association is founded.

1965

The first Head of the Charles, now the biggest U.S. regatta, is held in Cambridge.

1966

The National Rowing Foundation is established to support USRowing.

1969

John Fairfax (rowing westward from the Canary Islands to Miami) and Tom McClean (rowing eastward from Newfoundland to Ireland) each complete the first solo transatlantic crossings.

1970

The first World Youth Championships in Greece.

1972

Title IX of the Omnibus Education Act is passed It will effective y change women's rowing (and all sports) in America over the next generation.

1973

The U.S. enters its first national women's quad in the European rowing championships.

1974

Kent School crew coach Hart Perry is the first foreigner elected a Henley steward.

Rowing News, **April 1967.** Courtesy of the National Rowing Foundation and *Rowing News*.

1976

The Montreal Olympics hosts the first-ever Olympic women's events. The U.S. women win silver (single) and bronze (eight).

The Yale women's crew makes rational news by stripping in the athletic director's office to protest for better treatment and facilities.

1980

Philadelphia Rowing for the Disabled, the first adaptive rowing program in the United States, is founded.

1997

Women's rowing becomes a National Collegiate Athletic Association Sport.

2004

The U.S. men's eight wins gold and the U.S. women's eight takes silver at the Athens Olympics.

3: THE RIGHT STUFF

Equipment for Rowers

The list of equipment for rowers is not extensive, but it can be very expensive. The most important piece of equipment—the boat, or "shell"—can cost anywhere from $25,000 and up for an eight-person boat. Single boats, referred to as "sculls," range in price from $2,500 to $7,000 and higher.

Fortunately, thanks to the enormous growth of the sport over the last few years, a great deal of excellent used equipment is available today. For example, many of the top collegiate teams sell their equipment after just three years of use. This creates a great opportunity for a fledgling club team or a scholastic crew to acquire a quality boat or boats at a good price. Then, if the boat is well cared for, it can easily be used for another ten or fifteen years.

THE SHELL

Many crews have favorite brands of boats they want to row and proudly display in their boathouses. Pococks, made on the West Coast, have been around for decades and are still the preeminent brand of durable wooden

The Herrick shell, named for early twentieth-century Harvard coach Robert F. Herrick.

shells. Vespoli and Resolute synthetic shells are also very popular these days.

As much as some crews swear by their boatbuilders, no shell comes with a guarantee that those who row it will win a championship. Brad Woodrick, the boatman who meticulously cares for the Princeton crew's equipment, agrees that excellent gear is a plus for any crew, but he insists it's the oarsmen who really count. "If you've got a big strong crew, you're going to go fast!"

Even George Pocock, the famous American boatbuilder whose wooden shells dominated the rowing market for most of the twentieth century, concurred: "There is no such thing as fast boats, only fast crews."

Up until the mid-1970s, wood was the material of choice for racing shells. High-quality

The Oxford 1829 eight-oared shell was 45 feet (13.75 m) long and weighed 600 pounds (272 kg) —nearly two and a half times the weight of a modern eight.

Handle with care: Yale rowers take their shells to water.

boats were most often a combination of several different kinds of wood, such as spruce, mahogany, cedar, and ash. Today, wooden boats are still built and rowed, but more often shells are made of materials such as honeycombed carbon fiber, especially if they are intended for racing. Today's shells appear whisper-thin and light, but they are tough and durable in the water.

Regardless of how they are made, shells are named for the number of rowers they hold. The terminology is slightly different when describing sweep boats (a multiperson boat in which rowers use only one oar and row on one side), as opposed to sculling boats (with a rower or rowers each using one oar on each side).

USRowing's general requirements for boats:

A boat in the sport of rowing shall have all its load-bearing parts, including the axes of moving parts, firmly fixed to the body of the boat, but the seat of a rower may move along the axis of the boat.

The use of "sliding riggers," in which the fulcrum of the oar is not stationary with respect to the body of the boat, is strictly forbidden, except that the local organizing committee may allow such equipment if the event is clearly publicized as "experimental," and if all teams are informed in writing in advance that such equipment will be allowed in that event.

Categories of Boats

# Rowers	Oar	Coxswain	Min. Weight (lbs./kgs.)
1	scull	without 1×	30.86/14
2	scull	without 2×	59.53/27
2	sweep	without 2–	59.53/27
2	sweep	with 2+	70.55/32
4	sweep	without 4–	110.23/50
4	sweep	with 4+	112.44/51
4	scull	without 4×	114.64/52
4	scull	with 4×+	116.85/53
8	sweep	with 8+	205.03/93
8	scull	with 8×	213.85/97

For purposes of above minimum weights, the boat shall not include oars, or detachable loudspeaker or electronic systems. Seats, rudders, skegs, fins, and riggers shall be included in the boat's weight. Other items that are not permanently affixed to the boat shall not be included in the boat's weight.

THE MOVING PARTS

The mighty shell gets all the glory, but even the sleekest of racing boats would just bob in the water if it weren't for the rest of the rower's equipment. It takes an oar (or two oars, for scullers) to make the shell go.

OARS

Oars (never say "paddles"!) move boats through the water and serve to balance them. Sweep oars are longer than sculler's oars (also called *sculls*) and have wooden handles instead of rubber grips. The shaft of the oar, which, like the shell, used to be made of wood, is today made of extremely lightweight carbon fiber.

Like most rowing equipment, oars can be pricey. But again, there are plenty of used oars floating around that can be had for $100 or less.

The oar's design has evolved over the years, but these days most rowers use so-called hatchet blades, named for their cleaverlike shape.

Stow away: Rowers carefully store their essential equipment.

Push-off: A crew uses its oars to get things started.

These blades have a large surface area, almost 20 percent larger than previous blades.

The oars are attached to the boat with riggers, which provide a fulcrum for the levering action of rowing. Usually, sweep rowers sit in configurations with the oars alternating from side to side along the boat. Sometimes, the coach will rig the boat so that two consecutive rowers have their oars on the same side, in order to balance the boat (known as *German rigging*).

Crews are often identified by their oar blade design. Think of the red of Harvard or the red and blue of the USA National Team.

Regarding race day, USRowing Rules say:

Oars, whether sweep or scull, must be uniform throughout the crew, except that each rower in a composite crew may use the colors of his or her own club. Only the national or club colors may appear on oar blades. Unpainted oars are also permitted for all boats, whether composite or otherwise, if all rowers use such oars. Use of National Team colors without the express approval of USRowing is specifically prohibited.

Also:

The blade of an oar shall have the following minimum thickness: sweep oar, 5mm. [0.2 inch] (measured 3mm. [0.12 inch] from the tip of the blade); scull oar, 3mm. [0.12 inch] (measured 2mm. [0.08 inch] from the tip of the blade).

SLIDES

In the 1870s, it was discovered through much trial and error that oarsmen could gather more power and move faster if they were able to use their legs during the stroke, courtesy of a sliding seat. The real advantage of a moving seat comes from the fact that the oar is attached to a moving pivot instead of a stationary hinge.

TIPS FOR OAR MAINTENANCE

Adjust handles. Many rowers using adjustable oars keep the handle set at the same position, so it is likely that they will become stuck if they are never adjusted. To prevent this, every week or so, loosen the handle clamp bolt and slide the handle in and out a few times.

Prevent rust. Every once in a while, apply a waterproof spray lubricant to all metal surfaces.

Check for damage. Every so often, inspect your oars for damaged parts. Look especially at the blade, because catching and repairing slight damage will prevent more serious or irreversible damage.

Race-day equipment at the ready.

> ## "Oarsmen, I believe, develop a fluid joint in their pelvic girdles to adapt to varying seat configurations."
> —STEPHEN KIESLING, *The Shell Game*

The *slide* (seat, wheels, and track) has evolved over the years to its current configuration, which includes silent nylon wheels, which are mounted on ball bearings and glide inside two parallel stainless steel tracks.

Rowers also speak of "the slide" when referring to the seat itself and their use of it, as in "shooting the slide."

One size fits most: Today's stretchers are really big shoes.

STRETCHERS

Footstretchers, or "stretchers," are the adjustable footrests where rowers place their feet. Although some shells are still equipped with leather flaps and shoelaces, much like those used decades ago, most stretchers these days are actual athletic shoes. Usually, the shoes are big enough to accommodate almost any foot. Also, when they are first put in place, they are slit in half and then patched together with Velcro so rowers can easily rip their feet out if the boat capsizes (very important for safety).

Stretchers are a crucial piece of equipment: if rowers' feet were not secured, they would drive themselves off the end of the slide and have no way to pull themselves back.

Since the shoes stay in the boat (rowers don't take them on and off), oarsmen don't really need "rowing shoes," they just need shoes to get them to and from the boat. This is why, when a crew is out on the water, a big pile of shoes on the dock is a common sight.

USRowing Rules say:

Where the feet of the competitor are held in place by footgear affixed to the structure of the boat, the design of such footgear shall provide for the quick release of the competitor's feet in case of emergency, without the use of hands. Any pull strings shall not allow the heel to raise more than three inches (7.5 cm) above the foot board to which it is anchored.

RIGGERS

A *rigger* is the person, also called a *boatman*, who takes care of a crew's boathouse and equipment and often travels to races. Since only well-funded rowing programs (such as those at prep schools, large universities, and the national teams) can afford to pay a full-time rigger, it's often the coach or a member of the crew who plays this role.

A *rigger* is also an important piece of equipment: a set of metal or carbon fiber tubes that are affixed to the gunwale of a shell for the oarlock and gate. Riggers, which extend from the hull at each seat, consist of a backstay, a stem, and sometimes a forestay.

A boatman's work is never done.

EVOLUTION OF MODERN ROWING EQUIPMENT

A row, row, row of boats—every rower's dream.

1828

A form of outrigger for racing boats is developed by Anthony Brown of Newcastle-on-Tyne, England.

1844

A racing single with outriggers and an inboard keel makes its appearance on the Thames.

Sculling in the 1800s could be a ticket to stardom. Courtesy of the National Rowing Foundation.

1856

Oxford introduces a smooth bottom, as opposed to the former heavy keel—the beginning of the modern shell.

1857

J.C. Babcock of New York adapts a form of slide for a single. In 1870, he will outfit a six with slides. (Others, including the famous sculler Ned Hanlan, have also been credited with a similar invention around the same time.)

1868

"Guts" Woodgate introduces the coxless-four boat at Henley after devising a foot-steering mechanism and having the coxswain leap out after the start.

1873

For the first time, both Oxford and Cambridge use sliding seats in the Boat Race.

1875

Pro oarsman Michael Davis patents the swivel oarlock.

1876

Davis patents a sliding rigger.

1880

Davis patents a steering footstretcher, as well as the "Leg-o-Mutton" blade, a predecessor to the contemporary hatchet shape.

1912

The Pococks begin building racing shells in their Seattle boat shop.

1959

The tulip blade is popularized at the European Championships.

1960

Oxford introduces spoon oars to the Boat Race.

1972

German manufacturer Empacher Bootswerft successfully uses composite materials to advance shell construction.

1977

The Dreissigackers, rowers who started the company that is now Concept2, introduce light, durable oars made of composite materials.

1978

Richard Kellerman, a chemist at Xerox, and his associate Paul Nielsen establish Nielsen Kellerman and introduce the Cox-Box amplifier/stroke meter timer.

1980s

Vespoli boats become the standard choice for most American crews.

1981

Concept2 ergometers (rowing machines) are introduced.

1984

Nielsen Kellerman introduces the StrokeCoach stroke meter, designed for scullers and straight boats, enabling them to know their stroke rate and time even without a coxswain on board.

1991

Hatchet oar blades are introduced by the Dreissigackers.

THE GEAR

CLOTHING

Rowers, like all athletes, need their clothing to be practical. Since oarsmen spend so much time outside, often in very cold conditions, layering is key.

Most rowers wear shorts, leggings, or full-body unitards made of microfibers, such as polypropylene or nylon (spandex), that move easily and wick sweat away from the body. Snug but stretchy material is ideal because it doesn't get caught in the slide, the seat tracks, or other parts of the boat. Cotton T-shirts are okay, but they tend to get and stay wet, so microfiber tops are best. Jackets and sweatshirts made of fleece or other light but warm fabrics work well on the water.

In the chilly days during spring and fall, especially in the Northeast, oarsmen will want to wear hats and socks made of wool or moisture-resistant material. Some rowers will want to wear gloves, although that is often frowned upon for two reasons: one, wearing gloves keeps calluses from forming, which oarsmen need to build up to prevent blisters; and,

Best dressed: layering and comfort are key.

two, your teammates may accuse you of being less than tough.

One option is to wear *poagies*, rower's gloves that cover both the hands and the oar handle so the oarsman can keep warm but still grip the handle with his bare hands. (They are made for both scullers and sweep rowers!)

Even during cool weather, rowers should wear plenty of sunscreen (minimum SPF15) and reapply it often. The sun's damaging rays can wreak havoc on skin, even on cloudy days.

Men and women dress mostly the same on the water. Gone are the early twentieth-century days when men would wear street clothes or even suits, and women, often just along for the ride, would wear long dresses and twirl lacy parasols. The biggest change in women's garb came during the initial surge in women's rowing during the early 1970s. The women on the first U.S. Women's National Team, the famous Red Rose Crew, made a splash at the 1975 World Championships wearing bright-red, sleeveless leotard tops and very short shorts. According to Daniel Boyne, the author of *The Red Rose Crew*, they were self-conscious wearing the outfits that were so different from the

THE BUZZ

The introduction of the famous crew-cut hairstyle is largely credited to early 1940s Yale and Harvard crews, whose members decided it showed camaraderie, intensity, and practicality.

A story told by Yale alumni credits one of their own, John Hay "Jock" Whitney, with setting the trend when he walked into a New Haven barbershop in 1926 and asked for a "Hindenburg" haircut, resembling the short hair worn by German soldiers in World War I. As the legend goes, the barber said, "We just fought a war with those guys. I can't call it that."

Jock responded, "Just make it as short as you can. I'm rowing for the crew."

THE SHIRT OFF MY BACK

It is customary in rowing for the losers of a competition to give their racing shirts to the victors—each member of the losing crew gives his shirt to his counterpart (the bow, stroke, six seat, etc.).

Rowers are also famous for trading shirts during international competitions and bringing home memorable souvenirs.

Team garb for a rower's most loyal fans.

baggy gym shorts and T-shirts worn by most crews of the day. As it turned out, they were about 20 years ahead of their time.

That covers practice. But USRowing Rules are more specific about race-day uniforms:

All competitors in a crew shall wear identical clothing. Such clothing shall cover the torso of the body and may include sweatgear. The Chief Referee may grant exceptions to this rule on account of unusual weather conditions.

Individual competitors in a crew may choose whether or not to wear a hat or other headgear, which may be of the individual competitor's own choosing and need not be identical with those worn by other crew members.

THE BOATHOUSE

If there is a mecca for rowers in the United States, it is probably Philadelphia's Boathouse Row, where boathouses of legendary crews from Vesper to the Schuylkill Navy sit on the banks of the Schuylkill River. It's an impressive sight, especially when the buildings are lit up at night.

Philly's famous Boathouse Row.

Princeton crews
and U.S. National
Team rowers launch
from the Bernard
Shea Rowing Center
on Lake Carnegie
in Princeton,
New Jersey.

No less impressive (and no less a rower's mecca) is Boston's Charles River and its many famous boathouses, such as Harvard's Newell and Weld boathouses and the Riverside Boat Club, among many other collegiate and club headquarters. And then there's the Pocock boathouse on the shores of Lake Washington, where most of America's rowing fleet was built from 1920 to 1970.

Every crew aspires to have a boathouse filled with shells stacked on racks and a state-of-the-art training room, complete with an indoor rowing tank and rows and rows of ergometers (rowing machines called "ergs" for short). Some crews have one (or more than one, as is the case with Harvard and Yale, which each keep an additional boathouse in New London, Connecticut, just to train for the annual race against each other). Some crews do not.

But as wonderful as it is to have a boathouse to call home, a crew, especially a new one, doesn't have to have its own digs in order to row. Many scholastic crews form relationships with colleges or clubs and arrange to share facilities and equipment. Some collegiate crews share boathouses, as do many club crews.

So a crew should never let the lack of a roof over its head keep it off the water.

RIGGING AND MAINTENANCE

More than almost any sport, the equipment involved in crew is nearly as important as the athletes themselves. And more than almost any sport, it is up to the athletes to be responsible for their equipment. Although novice rowers and scholastic crews will always have coaches, riggers (if they're lucky), and more experienced teammates to help with the technical aspects of maintaining a boat, it is each rower's responsibility to make sure his boat is working well and ready to row.

In the 1970s, many women in new collegiate programs rowed in the big, heavy shells that had been discarded by a male crew. They often compensated for the too-big boats by attaching blocks of wood to the feet so they could take full strokes.

All crews have different systems, but almost always, especially on a scholastic level, each crew is responsible for its own boat. That means storing it, caring for it, transporting it (or readying it for transport), and rigging it. A large chunk of crew practice often consists of working on the boats—removing the riggers so the boats can be transported to a weekend competition and stacking the boats on the trailer, for example.

It makes sense that rowers take responsibility for their individual sections of the boat. Who better to determine whether stretchers and seats are adjusted correctly than the rowers themselves? Each rower should keep all moving parts near his seat clean and well lubricated, and notify the coach of any problems. (Better to be safe than sorry on race day!)

Naturally, rowers are also responsible for their own oars. Most oarsmen have a favorite oar, and often use the same one all season, so taking care of it by regularly greasing the button and storing it properly is common sense.

As part of its excellent coaching education program, USRowing offers many resources on rigging. One of the best, "Basic Rigging," was

On the Move

Traveling to regattas is a big part of any crew's season, and getting there safely and with the equipment intact is the main goal. Driving a trailer stacked with 60-foot (18.25-m) shells is not as easy as driving a car. The driver should be experienced, and the trailer should be insured.

Here are a few other useful road trip tips:

■ Planning is key. It's helpful to make a diagram with steps to follow when loading the trailer for a trip. Also, familiarize yourself with the route you will take (including clearance of bridges, etc.), and be sure to park where you won't be blocked in when it's time to depart.

■ Check the trailer for problems (tire pressure, etc.) before it is loaded.

■ Load the shells with the bow pointed toward the tow vehicle.

■ Secure everything. Immobilize the seats (or crate them), tighten footstretchers, and lash down oars and riggers.

■ Tie flags on the bow and stern (or a string of lights, for night travel) for better visibility.

■ Balance the load, and don't overload the trailer.

■ Attach safety chains to hold the trailer to the vehicle in the event the trailer comes off the hitch.

Rowers and riggers—often one and the same.

written by Mike Vespoli, the former Olympic rower, coach of the freshman Yale crew and owner of Vespoli racing shells. We've included it as an appendix so you can refer to it when you're ready to rig your own boat—or when you just want to understand better how a boat works.

Equipment: Any part of a boat, oar, or other mechanism that is used in the normal propulsion, flotation, or steering of a boat.

SWEEP BOATS

Eight: An eight-oared shell is the largest rowing shell. It carries eight sweep rowers and is always rowed with a coxswain. Eights are on the order of 58 to 62 feet [17.7 to 18.9 m] long and may weigh in the range of 200 to 300 pounds [90.7 to 136 kg], depending on the composition of the shell and its age. The eight (abbreviated: 8+) is the fastest boat on the water.

Four: A four-oared shell holds only four sweep rowers and may or may not have a coxswain. With a coxswain, a four is referred to as a "four with" (4+). Fours without a coxswain are referred to as "straight fours" (4−).

Pair: A pair is the smallest sweep boat, with only two rowers, and is considered the most difficult to row. As with fours, a pair may or may not be rowed with a coxswain. A pair with a coxswain is called a "pair with" (2+), while a pair without a coxswain is called a "pair without," a "straight pair," or a "coxless pair" (2−).

Scullers doing double duty on the Charles River.

SCULLING BOATS

Double sculls: Built for two scullers, the double is similar to a pair; in fact, the same shell can be used as a pair or a double by changing the riggers. Doubles are usually rowed without a coxswain and designated as merely a "double" (2×+).

Quadruple sculls: Usually referred to as a "quad," this is the largest sculling shell used in crew racing. The same shell can be used for a four or a quad by changing the riggers. As with a four, it can be rowed with or without a coxswain. If rowed with a coxswain, it is called a "quad with" (4×+). Rowed without a coxswain, it is called a "straight quad" (4×−).

Single scull: Built for one sculler, the single is the smallest racing shell. A single is around 26 feet [8 m] long and may weigh on the order of 28 to 38 pounds [12.75 to 17.25 kg]. Singles are designated as "1×" and are never rowed with a coxswain.

SHELL PARTS

Bow: The forward end of the shell, which goes through the water first.

Bow ball: The rubber ball situated at the end of the bow and designed to prevent boats from tearing holes in each other should there be a collision. It should be white or fluorescent in color and at least 4 centimeters (1.6 inches) in diameter.

Bow clip: The piece of plastic located near the front of the bow deck that holds the bow number during a race.

Bow deck: The forward section of the boat, in front of the bowperson.

Center pin: Located in the center of the footstretcher near the bottom of the shell, the center pin helps to hold the footstretcher in place.

Footstretchers: Also called *bootstretchers*, these are the holders where rowers place their feet. Some footstretchers are made of wooden clogs with leather slides, while newer shells are equipped with shoes. The footstretchers are adjustable toward the stern or bow of the shell, depending on the height of the rower.

Gunwale: Pronounced "gunnel," this is the upper edge of the side of the boat.

Hull: The bottom of the shell; the frame or body of the shell.

Keel: The piece extending along the entire length of the bottom of the boat and supporting the frame. All wood boats have keels; most plastic shells do not have a keel.

Keel strip: Also called the *center strip*, it is what the center pin attaches to. It also allows the footstretcher to be adjusted toward the stern or bow.

Knockers: In wooden boats, the wooden pieces attached to the tiller cables that the coxswain holds. Some coxswains use the knockers to bang on the side of the boat to help the crew hear the count or to keep cadence. This practice should be discouraged as it weakens the integrity of the shell's skin. In plastic boats, the wooden knockers have been replaced with rubber or plastic balls.

All rowing boats may be called shells. Rowing boats carrying scullers (where each person has two oars) are called sculls. So, all sculls are shells, but not all shells are sculls.

Port: The left side of the boat, facing forward (from the coxswain's perspective).

Ribs: The curved crosspieces extending from the keel to the top of the hull, forming the framework of the boat.

Rudder: The movable piece of plastic or wood located below the waterline beneath the stern of the boat, and used for steering.

Rudderpost: The metal post to which the rudder is attached.

Seat clips: The metal or plastic pieces that hold the sliding seat close to the tracks and prevent it from jumping off the tracks.

Side pins: Located on both sides of the footstretcher, the side pins hold the footstretchers in place.

Side tracks/ holes: Located on both sides of the footstretcher, the side tracks are what the side pins attach to. Different holes allow the footstretchers to be adjusted forward and aft.

Skeg: The plastic or metal fixed fin, located near the stern of the shell, which helps keep the shell on a straight course.

Skin: The outer covering of a wood shell, usually made of cedar.

Sliding seat or slide: Where the rower sits. The seat has small wheels that run on or in tracks.

Sling: The portable, folding stands used to hold the boats during rigging or whenever the boat is out of the water and off the racks.

Starboard: The right side of the boat, facing forward (from the coxswain's perspective).

Stern: The rear end of the shell.

Stern deck: The rear section of the boat, located behind the coxswain.

Tiller: The metal bar on top of the rudderpost, used to move the rudder.

Tiller cables/ ropes: The metal cables or nylon ropes that attach to the tiller and are used by the coxswain to maneuver the rudder and steer the boat.

Tracks: Sometimes referred to as the "slide" or "runners," the tracks are the grooved strips of metal or plastic upon which a sliding seat travels backward and forward. At each end of the tracks are the "stops," which prevent the wheels from running off the tracks.

Washboard: Also called a *splash guard*, the washboard is located behind the bow person's seat; this piece of wood or plastic prevents water from spilling into the boat.

OAR PARTS

Blade: The broad flat part of the oar located at the end of the oar shaft that is pulled through the water. The front of the blade is called the "face" of the blade. Blades are painted with the club colors of the crew.

Button: Also called the *collar*, this plastic piece divides the outboard or blade end of the shaft from the inboard end and prevents the oar from slipping through the oarlock.

Face of button: The surface of the button closest to the blade end of the oar.

Handle: Also called the *grip*, sweep oar handles are made of wood. Sculling oar handles are covered with rubber grips.

Right on the button.

Inboard length: The distance from the end of the oar handle to the face of the button. Inboard length is usually the spread measurement plus about a foot (30 cm, plus or minus 2 cm).

Oar: Made of plastic or wood, the oar is what a rower uses to propel a rowing shell. Sweep oars are around 12 feet, 6 inches (381 cm) in length, while sculling oars are around 9 feet, 6 inches (289.5 cm).

Oar length: The overall distance from the tip of the blade to the tip of the handle.

Outboard length: The distance from the tip of the blade to the face of the button.

Shaft: Also called the *loom*, this is the main body of the oar.

Sleeve: The plastic covering on the shaft of the oar on which the button is located.

> In the past, when an oar broke, the rower took it home and hung it (somewhat) proudly over his mantel. The custom is practiced less often thanks to the virtually indestructible composite oars used today.

4: How to Row

The ABCs of Moving a Boat

Common sense dictates that a person who wants to learn to row needs to do more than just read a book or look at pictures. The only way to really learn is by hitting the water. The only way to improve is by hitting the water as often as possible. But it helps to visualize what you're striving for and to know a few basic things before leaving the dock.

BRINGING THE BOAT TO WATER

It takes teamwork to hoist a shell.

Big boats such as eights, fours, and even sometimes pairs are too heavy for one person to carry. Shells are stored upside down on the racks, so some caution is in order when lifting them down. Always support the boat in the middle—it's a bad idea to grab it just by the ends, as that will put too much stress on the middle of the boat.

Smaller shells such as single sculls can be carried alone. According to Daniel Boyne, author of *Essential Sculling*, if a boat is stored below waist level on the racks, you need to grab the riggers or the gunwales to lift the boat and roll it right side up. Then, supporting the shell with your knee or a sling, switch your grips to the inside of the boat.

Conversely, Boyne says, if the boat is stored higher than waist level, reach in and grab the handholds. Rest your hands on the seat deck as you do this and keep your fingers wrapped around the handle or portals. Then lift the shell up slightly, tilt it toward you, and walk it away from the rack.

Next, carry your scull to the dock by hoisting it above your head and resting it on your head or on one shoulder.

Bigger boats are carried much the same way—brought down from the racks and down the docks to the beat of a coxswain's commands—but in this case, many hands (or heads and shoulders) make light work.

After a crew lowers the boat into the water, half the rowers return to the boathouse to fetch the oars.

Since a sculler is a one-man show, he brings his oars down first and then transports his shell to the dock. Once at the water's edge, he rolls the boat over and gently lowers it onto the surface.

When time to leave the water, follow a lasting tradition: from the first novice practice to a medal-winning performance in the Olympics, every crew always carries its boat back to the rack.

All in a (wet) day's work.

Way enough!

SHELL CARE

■ Always store boats upside down on racks so all the water drains out and the shell stays dry.

■ When taking a shell off the rack to work on the rigging, have a set of slings at the ready where you can safely mount it.

■ When transporting a boat, don't hold it by the ends unless that's where the handles are placed.

■ Consider buying a boat with removable rigging. This makes it lighter and easier to store and transport.

■ When carrying shells alone, have someone spot you, if possible, especially the first few times you do it.

■ Always make sure you have a good grip on the boat so you won't drop it.

■ Figure out which way is most comfortable for you to carry the boat to ensure you don't injure your neck or back.

■ If your boathouse has low ceilings or archways, use the shoulder carry.

COMING AND GOING

When it's time to climb on board, the most important thing for rowers to remember is this: do not step directly into the bottom of the boat. Ever. This will do serious damage to the boat no matter what material it's made of.

Everyone has to find his own style for entering and exiting his shell. (Warning: At first, it's never graceful!)

When it comes to big boats, especially eights, rowers strive to climb aboard in a very orderly fashion. First, each crew member stands by his seat, then the coxswain commands their movements: the starboard (odd-numbered) seats hold the gunwale while the port (even-numbered) seats, holding their oars with one hand, fully extend their oars out over the water and then step into the shell right foot first, taking care to put their weight on a sturdy cross-member of the boat, not the bottom. Next, ports put their left feet into the stretchers and take their seats. Then the starboards put their respective oars in one hand, step in, and sit while the ports hold the dock. The coxswain enters the shell last.

The maneuver is somewhat more challenging for a single, since the rower doesn't have other already seated comrades to hold the boat steady. For scullers, Daniel Boyne (*Essential Sculling*) recommends a move

DOS AND DON'TS

Don't step into the hull. (Your foot could push through the bottom of the boat.)

Do step on the platform.

Don't use the gunwales for support.

Do grab the rigger arm or the oarlock pin.

Party of one.

that resembles a one-legged knee bend. First, the rower holds on to both oar handles with the hand nearest the water, then pushes the sliding seat toward the bow with his other hand or foot. Next, he steps into the sternmost center section of the seat platform, directly in between the seat tracks.

NOTE: Many boats actually have a step plate or at least a textured skid pad indicating where the foot should go.

Then, before lowering himself onto the seat, he checks that it has returned to a position just behind his heel. When he bends at the knee, he also bends at the waist to maintain balance. His free foot can swing directly to the footboard, where it rests lightly while his free hand helps support his weight by resting on the dock.

There are other methods, of course, such as simply sitting down on the dock and, essentially, shuffling onto the seat. The most important thing, whether entering a single or an eight, is to always keep hold of the oar handles to stabilize the boat. (The same holds true for getting out.)

LAUNCHING

Launching from the dock is relatively easy. To launch a single scull, hold both oar handles with your left hand, then push away from the dock as smoothly as possible with your right foot. When the inboard rigger clears the dock, slowly sit down in the seat. Make sure the inboard rigger has cleared the edge of the dock and that the shell is a safe distance from other boats; then you can take a few strokes, adjust the slide, and get settled in the boat.

TIP FOR SCULLERS: Try not to leave from the dock going sideways, which could put you out of balance. Aim to move away from the dock in a forward/diagonal direction while slightly squaring your waterside oar.

In larger boats, the crew usually pushes away from the dock in a similar fashion, moving together per the coxswain's commands. But to a great degree, it depends on the docking situation (How large is the dock? Are there other boats present?) and the team's preference. Some crews push off with their feet, then get seated. Some have half the boat get in while the others push off. Some get in and "walk it down,' each rower

A sculler calls it a day.

Perfect landing.

grabbing the dock with his free hand to move the boat past the end of the dock. Trial and error (ideally, not too much error) is the best approach.

LANDING

Landing (returning to the dock) is a bit more challenging, but will get easier with practice. Remember, you need more power coming in against the wind and less coming in with it. Also, it's important to stop rowing when you are several lengths away from the dock so you can slow down and avoid a crash.

When a single sculler approaches the dock, he should stop rowing and push his oar handles down in his lap, then lean away from the dock so the shell will slowly begin to pivot on the waterside blade while the other oar lifts up over the dock.

MAKING WAY

Whether oarsmen row for fun, for exercise, or to hone their competitive edge, one thing always remains the same: the stroke.

THE STROKE CYCLE

The stroke cycle consists of the same four-part sequence performed over and over in the same order—catch, drive, finish, and recovery. This is true for both sculling and rowing sweep boats.

1. Catch. The beginning of the stroke when the blade enters the water. The rower is fully compressed (knees bent, arms reaching forward) and up the slide. The blade is fully squared (perpendicular) to the water.

This is the opposite of the finish.

2. Drive. The part of the stroke when the blade is in the water and the rower applies power to the oar. This consists primarily of the leg drive, then straightening the back, and finally pulling in the arms.

3. Finish (or Release). The end of the stroke when the blade is removed from the water. This is the opposite of the catch.

4. Recovery. The part of the stroke when the oar is out of the water and moving away from the finish to the catch. The rower begins with the hands away from the body during the finish, swings the upper body back to a slightly forward body angle position, then finally moves slowly back up the slide toward the catch.

Although the stroke cycle is broken into four parts when it is being discussed or taught, in practice, rowers move their oars in and out of the water in a continuous, fluid motion—there is no beginning or endpoint, much like a turning wheel.

In order to put the four parts together, as the stroke begins, the rower is coiled forward on the sliding seat, with his knees bent and arms outstretched. At the catch, he drops the oar blade vertically into the water. At the beginning of the drive, the alignment of the upper body doesn't change—the legs do all the work. As the upper body begins to uncoil, the arms begin their work, drawing the oar blades through the water. Continuing

CATCH TIPS

These tips are courtesy of Hartmut Buschbacher, U.S. Women's National Coach.

■ Square up early and keep the blades close to the water.

■ Keep the center of gravity on the seat in order to lift the handle easily and quickly.

■ Avoid diving at the catch to increase your reach, and don't push your legs before the blade enters the water.

■ The catch should be a light and effortless motion. Feel you are able to catch the speed of the boat right away and then immediately start to accelerate.

the drive, the rower moves his hands quickly in toward his body, which by this time is leaning back slightly. In this position, called *layback*, strong abdominal muscles are a plus.

During the finish, the rower moves the oar handle down, drawing the blade out of the water. At the same time, he "feathers" the oar—turning the oar handle—so that the oar blade changes from a vertical position to a horizontal one. The oar remains out of the water as the rower begins recovery, moving the hands away from the body and past the knees. The body follows the hands, and the sliding seat moves forward, until, knees bent, the rower is ready for the next catch.

Then he does it all again. And again. And again ...

The goal of every crew is to make rowing look easy. Rowers always strive for synchronization in the boat and a continuous, fluid motion, made up of clean catches and consistent speed. So, even though almost anyone can move the boat (however imperfectly) from the first hour on the water, getting it right takes a lot of practice and fine-tuning.

"There are ten actions that have to be performed simultaneously in an eight-oared boat. If you miss any one of them, the whole crew is out of balance—the least thing will put it out. You've got to have your hands all on one plane, you've got to catch right at the same time, you've got to pull through, you've got to slide, you've got to drive your legs down, you've got to turn a wrist—all exactly at the same time. It's a beautiful thing to watch when it's done right."—GEORGE POCOCK

FEATHERING

One of the first things an oarsman—whether a sculler or a sweep rower—needs to learn is *feathering* (also called *bladework*). Basically, feathering is the art of rotating the oar during the finish, after the rower moves the oar handle down and draws the oar blade out of the water. The goal is to change the position of the blade from a vertical position to a horizontal one (once it's out of the water) so it meets less wind and water resistance during recovery. Although feathering is similar in sculling and sweep rowing, there is one obvious difference: a sculler must feather two oars simultaneously, learning to rotate both his hands in a relaxed motion to accomplish this coordinated task. Sweep rowers, who row with one oar, feather by using only the inside hand to roll the oar handle. The outside hand simply provides leverage. Both sweep rowers and scullers should make sure their blades remain buried in the water until they are ready to feather. Also, it's important to start with a good, relaxed grip.

SWEEPS

U.S. Women's National Coach Hartmut Buschbacher recommends placing the hands about one and a half hand widths apart (just shy of shoulder width). The outside hand covers the end of the handle with all fingers and lightly pushes the handle against the oar-

MORE GRIP TIPS

Sweeps

"Think of 'holding' the oar handle, not 'grabbing' it. Having the correct grip will enable you to 'hang' your body weight on the oar handle and get the maximum out of each stroke."
—Mike Teti, U.S. Men's National Sweep Coach

Sculls

"Don't squeeze the handles. Hold the handle in the hand as you would a sparrow, so as not to smother it but also so it does not fly away."—Igor Grinko, U.S. National Sculling Coach

Both

"If one squeezes the hand, the wrist gets tight, so avoid squeezing the oar during both the recovery and the pull through."—Harry Parker

lock during the recovery while the inside hand takes over completely at the catch and the finish.

"The wider the grip, the heavier the load, but breathing and shoulder work are enhanced," Buschbacher says. "The smaller the grip, the lighter the transfer of power into the oar handle due to the decreased leverage, and the upper body will follow the arc of the handle even more closely."

Most important, the grasp should be light, with most of the pressure concentrated in the fingerpads, not in the thumbs and palms (no squeezing!). The thumb should be under the oar handle, which gives the rower more control than having it on top. It's also important to relax the shoulders and arms.

Interestingly, the actual feathering motion is the same regardless of hand speed, but it must be done quickly before the push-away begins, so the oarsman can relax on the recovery.

Put more simply, feathering consists of a roll of both wrists, the heels of the hands dropping away from the body while the fingers roll the handle around in a clockwise and then counterclockwise motion. Mastering this wrist movement can be a novice's biggest challenge.

Even though this may sound like a lot to process, the good news is that feathering fast becomes second nature to most rowers.

MORE TIPS ON TECHNIQUE

■ Keep your back as straight as possible without being stiff. (A bent back makes for a weak stroke.)

■ Keep the recovery more relaxed than the drive.

■ Shoot for a position where the handle is well below your ribs, and keep your chest full, but relaxed.

■ Let the back have only one joint—at the hips.

■ Feel the feet. Stay focused on the connection between your feet and the footboards during the drive, as well as through the finish and release. If your feet don't push off the footboards throughout the entire stroke, you interrupt the transfer of force and your body acts like an anchor, slowing down the boat.

■ Moving off the stretcher, push off the balls of your feet. Very few people can get power from their heels.

■ The slide should feel twice as long on the recovery as on the drive.

■ If someone watching you from another boat or onshore gives you feedback, listen to him. He has a better vantage point to see your stroke than you do.

Every stroke a rower takes requires constant moving and repositioning of the hands. When the oar is placed in the water at the catch, coaches will say, "Roll the hands over the ankles," meaning the hands roll clockwise in a gradual motion until the blade is square. The arms and hands are raised, and the blade is dropped into the water. Every stroke also requires constant awareness and repositioning of the body.

Preparing for the catch, scullers should have shins upright, arms extended, shoulders forward, head up, and back firm. Sweep rowers should have shins vertical, knees apart (so the outside arm fits through), body weight centered at the outside knee, outside arm and shoulder extended (following the arc of the handle so that the axis of the shoulders is almost parallel to the oar), and the inside arm straight and relaxed.

During the drive, the hands don't roll. Instead, the wrists lock up and the fingers clench the oar (but not too tightly!) as first the legs and back, then the arms, rip the blade through the water to the finish. That is a good way to remember the sequence: legs, back, and arms. Also remember, the shoulders should remain steady and move in a horizontal plane throughout the drive.

"The three R's of rowing are: rowing, rowing, and rowing." —STAN POCOCK

Recovery, which is very important since it consists of half the entire stroke, begins when the arms draw level or slightly past the body. At this point, the body should be still while the hands feather and press away until the arms are loosely extended. Finally, the shoulders and upper body rock forward from the hips, aiming for a full-body angle for the next catch.

Remember, all this happens in just a few seconds. With practice, the flow of the stroke will come.

Solo stroke.

What Not to Do

Catch a crab: This is the big no-no in rowing. It happens when a rower's blade enters the water at an angle instead of perpendicular, and the blade gets caught under the surface of the water (the way it looks when a fisherman nets a scrambling crab). A full crab is when the oar handle levels the rower and completely passes over his body. Oarsmen seek to avoid crabs at all costs because they can grind a surging shell to a halt or even eject a rower (literally) from the shell! Watch out for choppy conditions, when crabs are most likely. If you catch a crab, you should give the stroke up for lost, try to regain your composure, then return to rowing.

Dive: This happens when the blade plunges or digs too deeply into the water at the catch or on the drive. Rowers can avoid this by keeping in mind that proper blade depth is only the width of the blade, or a "blade full."

Lean: Many rowers make the mistake of leaning to try to compensate for a flaw in their stroke. This is not a good way to balance. The goal should be to keep over the keel.

Miss water: This refers to too much forward movement of the blade at the catch before it enters the water.

Sightsee: A coach will say a rower is sightseeing when he turns his head and looks out of the boat. It's the coxswain's job to watch; a rower's job is to row.

Sky: The common error where the blade is waved too high in the air (as a result of the rower dropping his hands) as it approaches the next catch.

Wash out: The opposite of diving. This occurs when the blade is not buried deep enough during the drive.

Rush the slide: This happens when an oarsman, eager to go faster, moves the slide too quickly toward the stern. It actually has the opposite of the intended result—it causes the forward acceleration of the boat to slow or stop.

Shoot the slide: This refers to putting the legs down before the blade enters the water, or not opening the back soon enough so that the legs go down but the oar does not move. A good remedy is to keep proper body control at the catch.

Flip or fall out of the boat: Doing so can be embarrassing or dangerous. Nonetheless, many coaches recommend taking a dip on purpose (usually in a single) when first learning to row so you can conquer your fear of flipping. Once you've flipped, the theory goes, you'll know what to expect and how to get back into the boat.

Wanted: the perfect stroke.

TIPPING TIPS

- Secure your glasses on your head with a cord so you don't lose them.
- For your first tip, make sure an experienced rower is nearby to instruct and help you.
- Keep your feet out of the stretchers.
- After tipping, slide the oars so they are parallel to the hull and flip the shell back over.
- Holding on to the shell, swim with it toward the nearest bank or back to the dock. Do not attempt to climb back in on the water. This could ruin the shell!
- Once on the dock, get back in the shell.

ACCIDENTAL TIPPING TIPS

Although flipping in singles or doubles will almost certainly happen at one time or another, flipping in big boats is rare. Nonetheless, rowers should be well versed in safety procedures. USRowing offers extensive safety tips and procedures on its safety bulletin (USRowing.org). Here are a few basic tips:

- Make sure your feet are out of the stretchers.
- Slide the oars until they are running parallel to the hull and flip it back over.
- If the dock is close, swim the boat to it.
- If the dock is not close, swim the boat to the nearest bank and wait for help.
- Never try to reboard the shell while in the water—you will damage it.
- If a boat is swamped—taking on water and in danger of sinking— do not leave it. Once flipped, it will serve as an emergency flotation device.
- If your boat is in distress or if there is a man overboard, use distress signals to communicate with other boats: wave your arms or a shirt above your head or raise an oar in the air.
- If a rower is injured, the coxswain will command, "Way enough! Hold water!" Stop rowing immediately and signal the coaching launch for help.

MORE SAFETY TIPS

■ When the water temperature is low, carry a life jacket and a cell phone (in a waterproof case attached to your boat).

■ Keep a life jacket in your boat when rowing without a coaching launch nearby.

■ Learn how to put on a life jacket while in the water.

■ Check out maps of local waterways to learn about traffic patterns and potential hazards.

■ If sudden winds come up, return to the boathouse or take a boat to the nearest shore and wait for the winds to calm.

■ Don't row in fog unless your visibility is at least 100 yards. If fog sets in while you are on the water, move slowly and be prepared to stop quickly. Use a cox box, horn, or whistle to advise other boats of your location. Follow the shore back to the dock.

■ Do not row in an electrical storm. Lightning detectors are inexpensive and can clip on your belt. If you are on the water and see lightning, hear thunder, or notice your hair standing on end with static electricity, head for the nearest shore and wait for the storm to pass.

TURN IT AROUND

In big boats, turning is largely done by the coxswain's steering and subsequent commands to the crew. When a boat needs to turn, rowers (usually on one side) should push their oar handles away from their bodies while the blade is in the water. The coxswain will usually instruct the rowers on the other side to row normally in order to spin the shell around.

COMING TO TERMS

Here is a list of rowing technique terms, courtesy of USRowing:

Hanging on the oar: Refers to keeping the arms straight and the body angle set for the first half of the drive.

Layback: The angle of the body at the release, usually 10 to 15 degrees past the perpendicular.

Body angle: The forward angle of the body at the catch, usually 30 to 35 degrees.

The mark: The spot on the rower's body toward which the oar handle is pulled at the finish of the drive. To "find your mark," sit in the release position and rest the oar blade in a square position just below the surface of the water. The place where your outside hand meets your body is your mark.

Feather: The motion of flattening the blade so that it is parallel to the water following the release of the blade from the water.

Roll up: Also called squaring up, this is the motion of squaring the blade from the feathered position before the blade enters the water. Sweep rowers usually roll up early, while scullers tend to use a "flip-catch" or late roll-up.

Hook: The motion of backing the blade down toward the water just before the oar drops into the water for the catch.

Set: The balance of the boat.

Swing: Swing is the hard-to-define feeling when the crew's movements are almost perfectly synchronized, enhancing its performance and the shell's speed.

Run or glide: The movement of the shell during the recovery. Also, the distance traveled by the boat during the recovery measured by the spacing between puddles.

Ratio: The amount of time blades spend out of the water compared to the amount of time they spend in the water. Crews strive for a two-to-one ratio (twice as long on the recovery as the drive); when the rate gets above 35 strokes per minute (SPM), the ratio approaches one to one. Don't spend less time on the recovery than on the drive.

Stroke rate: Also called the *cadence*, the stroke rate is the number of strokes per minute (SPM).

Stern check: A slowing or stopping of the boat just before or after the catch. This can be caused by rushing the catch or having a slow catch or not applying pressure quickly on the face of the blade.

Bladework: The motion of the blades. Common bladework problems are early or late roll-up, under- or oversquared blades, skying of the blade, missing water, digging deep, and washing out.

Puddle: The movement of the water created by the pull of the oar. The size of the puddle indicates how much energy an individual rower is expending.

Spacing: The distance between the 2 seat's puddle and where the stroke oar's blade enters the water. *Even spacing* means that the distance between the 2 oar's puddle and the stroke's catch on the next stroke is the same distance as between the previous puddles.

A sculler finds her mark.

Outside hand: The hand farthest from the rigger, used to take the oar out of the water at the release.

Inside hand: The hand closest to the rigger, used to feather and square the blade on the recovery.

Pick drill: A stroke in which the rowers sit up straight and use only their arms and hands, with no body swing or leg drive.

Flat slide: Also called *dead slide*, this is a stroke in which rowers only use their arm pull and body swing while keeping their legs locked down.

Quarter slide: A stroke in which the rowers come one-fourth of the way up the slide on the recovery.

Half slide: A stroke in which the rowers come half the way up the slide on the recovery. Body angle at half slide is the same as body angle at full slide.

Three-quarter slide: A stroke in which the rowers come three-fourths of the way up the slide on the recovery.

Full slide: A stroke in which the rowers come all the way up the slide to reach full leg compression and full length.

Length: Also called *reach*, refers to how far back the rower places his blade before taking the catch. Normally, the catch angle is 50 degrees past the perpendicular; the release, 35 degrees.

Stroke power: Refers to the amount of power or pressure the rowers are exerting. Rowers may think in terms of full pressure, three-fourths pressure, half pressure, and so on, or they may row by percentages of full power.

On the paddle: Rowing with no power.

Wash: The creation of water turbulence that affects the progress of a crew.

5: TRAINING TOUGH

Workouts on the Water and in the Gym

"Mom, I want to join the crew."

For a parent who has only a passing acquaintance with rowing, these can be unsettling words.

A mom or dad's first thoughts may be of long, cold early morning drives to the boathouse or the maintenance of expensive equipment. (Will we need a trailer hitch?) But the more a parent or potential rower learns about the sport, the more the positives seem to outweigh the negatives.

According to Allen Eubanks, coach of the Oak Ridge Rowing Association varsity women, being a part of a crew is similar to participation in other sports. "It's a big commitment," he says. "Many crews practice five or six days a week. But the commitment is similar to baseball or football, and crews don't compete as much. We'll have maybe five races a year."

CREW PRACTICE AT A GLANCE

The best crew practices are well-organized and structured to make the best use of the athletes' and the coach's time. Since scholastic, junior, and collegiate crews consist of rowers who are also students, it's crucial to make practice time count.

'TIS THE SEASON

For the most part, practices are planned according to the season. In the fall, some rowers are brand new and the others are rusty, so fundamentals on the water are stressed, and basic weight training begins in the gym. Also, most crews emphasize endurance in the fall, as this is the season when many head *regattas* (long-distance races of one to three miles, such as the famous Head of the Charles in Boston) take place.

In the spring, crews that have been together all year will be more advanced in their drills and will row more frequent and intense *pieces* (short spurts of hard rowing that are often timed or set up as races between two crews). This, along with more focused training in the gym, prepares them for the short sprint style of racing and the regional and national championships that often take place in April, May, and early June.

A crew climbs on board for practice.

Spring practice on the Charles River.

The winter (due to the cold) and summer (due to school vacation) have traditionally been off-seasons for rowing, although that is changing with the growth of the sport, especially in the South. Crews in Florida, Texas, and California can continue to practice outside in the winter, whereas crews in Massachussetts, Ohio, and Wisconsin, whose rivers and lakes turn to ice, cannot.

So, during the winter, some rowers take a break from crew, perhaps participating in other sports. Or, more typically these days, crews train indoors in the gym, on ergometers (rowing machines that rowers call "ergs") and in indoor rowing tanks.

Although serious collegiate competitors and athletes bound for national teams have been making rowing a year-round activity since the 1950s, in the summer, with schools out of session, many crews disband until fall.

**Prepping the gear
is half the fun.**

Rowers are among the best athletes in terms of physical conditioning. (Long-distance speed skaters and cross-country skiers are comparable.)

But, again, due to the recent surge in popularity of rowing, the opportunities to row at camps and with club crews in the summer months are opening everywhere. Just follow the water.

PRACTICE PROTOCOLS

The countdown to crew practice signals a frenzy of activity. Athletes arrive at the boathouse or the dock and rush to ready themselves to row. They stow cell phones, backpacks, and shoes, and throw on extra layers of clothing if it's cold. Girls pull their hair into ponytails, and both boys and girls slather on sunscreen and don caps. The coach gives instructions to the coxswain, who will relay them to the crew, while the rowers attend to their equipment and warm up.

Every crew wants to spend the majority of its practice time on the water. Since this time is limited, many coaches get right to it. But everyone needs to warm up. Many coaches have rowers warm up on the ergs—just straightforward rowing for five to ten minutes at a low (in the 20s) stroke-per-minute rating.

Jaryn Finch, Brookline High School JV girl's crew coach, has her athletes row on the ergs to start. Then they often do this simple warm-up/stretch routine, which includes core strengthening and several yoga-inspired moves:

1. Sculling sit-ups. On the mat, sit upright, with legs extended in front of you, and your arms extended out to the side. Pull your knees to your chest, bringing your feet off the floor and your arms in for balance. Then, extend your legs in front of you, holding them off the floor, while extending your arms back out to the side. This mimics the position of a sculler. Do two sets of 30.

2. Hamstring stretch. With legs extended in front of you, bend forward at the waist and grab your ankles or the sides of your feet. Try to touch your chest to your thighs. Hold for 30 seconds.

3. Twisting stretch (abdominals and lower back). Sit up and fold your left leg underneath you. Cross the bent right leg over the top of your left leg and place your right foot next to your left knee. Keeping your hips facing forward, twist your body around to the right as far as you can without feeling pain. Keep your palms flat on the floor for support. Hold for 30 seconds. Repeat on the other side.

4. Plank. From a push-up position, extend your arms and rise up on your toes. Your back should be flat and your head aligned with your body, eyes looking down. Hold for 20 seconds.

5. Cobra. From the plank, lower your body down, flat on the floor, face down. Then, with palms flat and placed beside your shoulders, push just your upper body up, and stretch out with your chin lifted. Keep your lower body on the floor. Then lower your upper body to the floor, return to the plank position, and repeat the plank-cobra combination 10 times.

6. Downward-facing dog. From a push-up position, move your hands toward your feet so you raise your hips to form a triangle. Press your heels into the ground. Hold for 30 seconds. Repeat five times.

7. Cat. On all fours, move from a straight-back position to a full-rounded spine by bringing your chin to your chest. Return to a straight spine, then lift your head up to fully arch your back. Repeat 10 times.

8. Squats. Standing with legs shoulder distance apart and feet squared, inhale deeply and extend your arms straight in front of you. Squat down as far as you can without falling (aim for your ideal catch height in the boat). Try to keep the back straight. Repeat 10 times.

9. Waist bend. Standing up tall, extend your arms overhead and slowly reach them in front of you, bending at the waist. With legs straight, grab your ankles and hold for 30 seconds.

10. Stand tall. Extend your arms overhead, stand on your toes, spread out your fingers, and reach for the sky. Hold for 30 seconds.

NOTES ON STRETCHING

According to the American College of Sports Medicine, if done regularly and carefully, stretching can increase range of motion in the joints, nourish muscle tissue, improve coordination and posture, and contribute to improved athletic performance. That said, the current school of thought discourages stretching cold muscles. In other words, never start your workout by stretching. Only do it after a warm-up or, even better, after a full workout.

Although for years coaches and athletes believed stretching could prevent injury, there have been no conclusive studies published to prove this. However, most trainers find that stretching can help an athlete recover from an injury.

For a more detailed explanation of stretching, including diagrams of sample stretches, two good sources are the *Personal Trainer's Manual*, from the American Council on Exercise and *Stretching* by Bob Anderson (Shelter Publications).

TRAINING ON THE WATER

The best place to improve as a rower is on the water. Many novices start out rowing with a coach or a more experienced teammate in a *wherry*, a small craft with a sliding seat and short riggers, which was originally designed to row in rough waters and is much more stable than a typical racing shell. Other novices have good luck starting out rowing in a double, again with a more experienced rower. With just two oarsmen, it's easier to focus on how the new rower is performing.

Another great place to learn is in an indoor tank. *Tank* is another name for a narrow pool of water equipped with stable shells and surrounded by mirrors so a rower can check his form. In stationary tanks, athletes row using oars with hollowed-out blades that move through the water without moving the boat. In the more prevalent moving water tanks, where the water is pumped through in a continuous loop, coaches can easily adjust the rate of flow for different rowing speeds. Many of the movements that crews do on the water can be practiced alone or as a group in the tanks.

A tank is also a great place to break down the components of a stroke or to work on specific problems without distractions such as the wind or balance. More experienced rowers use the tanks for general conditioning. And coxswains like to spend time in the tanks so they can gain hands-on rowing experience and better critique other rowers. After a crew has the basics down, *then* it can hit the water.

Once they have pushed off from the dock, most crews would prefer to just head out and row. But in order to improve, rowers need to make time for drills. Here is a sample of popular training drills for coaches to run (courtesy of USRowing):

Pick drill. Instruct the rowers to sit up tall and row with their arms only, either on the feather or with square blades. This drill is good for practicing roll-up, catch-and-release timing, early roll-ups, and the down-and-around motion at the release. Also emphasize keeping pressure on the feet at the end of the drive and the beginning of the recovery.

Rowers tone their technique in the tanks.

Coaches map out practices in advance.

Flat slide. Instruct the rowers to keep their legs down and row with their backs (body swing) and arms (arm pull) only. This drill is good for timing, blade-work, and getting early body angle before the legs come up. Also emphasize keeping pressure on the feet at the end of the drive and the beginning of the recovery.

Quarter slide. While the rowers are rowing quarter slide, direct them to emphasize the last part of the drive and the first part of the recovery, especially the body swing into and out of bow and early body angle preparation, while bringing the legs up slow and controlled.

Half slide. Tell rowers rowing half slide, to emphasize having the body angle set by half slide, with the shoulders set and no lunge into the catch. This works on blade skills and quick catches.

Pause drills. These may be done rowing half slide with a pause at flat slide (start and stop at flat slide) or full-slide strokes, with one pause (at half slide) or two pauses (one at flat slide and another at half slide). Pause drills are good for emphasizing early body separation and controlling the slide early in the recovery.

Three-two-ones. Three flat-slide strokes followed by two half-slide strokes and one full-slide stroke, then repeat; or three flat-slide strokes followed by two quarter-slide strokes, then one half-slide stroke. This drill is good for bladework, timing, and developing swing.

Square blades, regular grip. Square blades is a good drill for both ends of the stroke, clean releases, and catches. At the release, empha-size the down-and-around motion to take the blade out. Especially stress that the outside hand and wrist stay flat even when feathering. This is also good for rowers who wash out during the drive.

Square blades, side grip. Instruct the rowers to place their inside hands down on the carbon and concentrate on squeezing the outside hand up and in. This is what keeps the outside shoulder up.

Outside hand only. Direct rowers to place the inside hand on the hip and row with the outside hand only. Use this drill only with square blades. The outside hand does not feather the blade—ever!

Inside hand only. Instruct the rowers to place the outside hand on the hip and row with the feathering inside hand. Emphasize the push-down and away while feathering.

Straight arms. Direct the rowers to keep their arms straight without breaking during the drive. Emphasize hanging on to the oar.

Oar placement drill. Tell the rowers to sit at release position with the blades squared and buried in the water. Then give them a command to come up the slide and place the blades in the water (catch) without starting the drive. This may be done by fours or all eight on flat, half, or full slide. Emphasize releases, balance and set, timing, and body position set at the catch.

> **Some coaches say when you're rowing and it starts to hurt, smile! Your brain will think you're enjoying it despite the pain.**

Plop or bounce drill. Instruct rowers to sit at catch position with blades squared and buried; command to lift the blades out and drop back in together. Emphasize the body set at the catch, no pressure on the handle, catching with the arms—lifting, not lunging—and rowing the blade in. Rowers should listen for the sound of the catch.

Cut the cake. This is an advanced bladework drill that involves an airstroke at half slide for every stroke taken. Emphasize the set of the boat during the airstroke.

Acceleration drill. Start with the stern pair and instruct them to row for five strokes, then add rowers 5 and 6 in for five strokes, then 3 and 4 for five strokes, and then the bow pair so that all eight are rowing. After all eight row five strokes, direct them to take the pressure up for ten strokes, then have them take the pressure and stroke rate up for ten more strokes. Repeat with 5 and 6 starting the drill, and so on. This excellent timing drill helps rowers feel the boat get lighter as it increases in speed.

Ten, ten, and tens. Can be done on half or full slide. Instruct all eight to take ten strokes at three-quarter pressure, then ten strokes at full pressure while increasing the rate, and then ten strokes taking the rate up as high as they can go. This is good for warming up before a race.

Five and glides. The coxswain counts out five power strokes; on the fifth stroke, the rowers come up to half slide and stop with the blades parallel to the water, allowing the boat to slide on the water. See how long rowers can balance the boat without having the blades hit the water, or use like the pause drills described above and have the rowers continue after a two- to three-second pause. This is an excellent drill for working on balance. Also, emphasize the use of the feet to set the boat and the feel of the boat running on the recovery.

Feet on top. Instruct the rowers to free their feet and place them on top of the footstretchers. While they row continuously, emphasize smooth motion around the corner at the release and constant contact with the feet on the footstretchers. This teaches proper layback position and good balance.

Eyes closed. Instruct rowers—except the coxswain!—to close their eyes. Tell the rowers to concentrate on balance, rhythm, and timing, and focus on relying on their sense of feel while listening to the boat.

TRAINING OFF THE WATER

ERGS

Although the next-best place (after the water) to perfect rowing form is in the tanks, many rowing drills can be mimicked on the ergs as well. The ergs are the best place to break down body positioning, as the rower is not dealing with any sort of boat or water.

Rowing machines, in their more rustic and rickety forms, have been around since the early 1800s. True ergometers, which consist of a

Take it inside: Ergs let rowers row year-round.

rolling seat, a flywheel (or a revolving drum with a resistance mechanism), an odometer to measure distance, and an oar handle attached to the flywheel by cable or chain, were first developed at Stanford University in the early 1960s. The Gamut ergs, which had more components to measure a rower's condition and progress, were introduced in the 1970s. Then in the 1980s, Concept II (now Concept2) changed rowers' lives forever by introducing the relatively inexpensive, more accessible models that we see in most gyms and boathouse training rooms today.

OUCH!

Blisters are the bane of any rower's existence. But they are absolutely inevitable and, to some degree, necessary, since after blisters follow the calluses rowers need.

While waiting for blisters to heal and calluses to form, it's best to take advice from experienced oarsmen on what works best (usually salves and ointments, along with gauze and tape). Hint: Wind long pieces of gauze (from a roll) around your hand and tape them down. This works better than trying to keep square gauze pads or Band-Aids in place.

Coaches often set up "test rows," using ergs to measure an athlete's progress by timing and recording his session. Rowers often begin selection camps for seats on national teams by hitting the ergs, often going head to head with other competitors in erg "races."

Erg racing even has its own event each year, when collegiate oarsmen meet to compete—on the ergs only for 2,000-meter [2,187.25-yard] indoor races—at the CRASH-B Sprints in Boston.

No question, erg rowing is one of the best aerobic workouts one can do. For that reason, many oarsmen hit the ergs to row for distance, pacing themselves for longer workouts to achieve as much cardio conditioning as possible. To further enhance endurance, rowers also use the ergs for quick rows, using short spurts of effort, resting, then performing the exercise again.

Brookline High School coach Jaryn Finch says she always tries to have her rowers spend at least part of every practice on the ergs. "I like them to work on the ergs at least for a short while every day so I have a guarantee of how much work they've done," she says.

On the ergs, the stroke breaks down much as it does on the water.

1. The catch begins when the body has stopped moving forward and is poised to drive backward. The abdomen should be flat against the top of the legs. The rower's head is erect, with eyes focused on the erg's tachometer.

2. In the drive, the knees push down and the back rises perpendicular to the floor. Arms stay rigid and straight, with the shoulders taking most of the pressure from the stroke. Three-quarters of the way through, the rower's back should lean past perpendicular while the legs flatten out. He pulls in the oar handle to finish the stroke.

3. For the finish, the rower tucks his elbows to his sides and pulls the handle into his stomach.

4. In the recovery, he extends his arms, bends his legs, leans forward slightly, and allows the wheel to pull the oar handle back to start.

After warming up or doing a straightforward cardio row, many coaches have the coxswain put the crew through erg training consisting of pause drills, during which

rowers pause after every finish to check their form. Often, rowers will do ten of these followed by ten fluid strokes so they can try to incorporate their good form into regular rowing. Then, for more endurance work, they will row at different SPMs, doing one minute at 18, two minutes at 20, three minutes at 22, one minute at 24, and so on.

AEROBIC TRAINING

Rowers at the turn of the century certainly didn't use the word "aerobic" while they were training. But as early as 1926, a British study of

Rowers get their hearts pumping on and off land.

oarsmen, published by the University of Durham, found that oxygen consumption increased with a higher stroke rate and that power increase leveled off as stroke rate rose because of the buildup of fatigue-causing lactic acid. The importance of physical conditioning on rowing performance took its greatest leap in the 1950s, when Karl Adam, a West German high school coach, began promoting theories of all-around physical conditioning, as well as year-round training. Harvard's Harry Parker took year-round training and conditioning to another level in the 1960s and 1970s. Today we are all believers.

The goal of off-the-water cardio training (on ergs or through other activities such as running, biking, or swimming) is to condition the body to postpone for as long as possible the switch from the aerobic state (where energy is supplied by oxygen) to the anaerobic state (where the body has consumed available oxygen and is forced to convert sugar and fat to energy).

Rowers need to have an enormous aerobic capacity; if they don't, they won't row for long. That's the reason, in addition to rowing on shells and rowing on ergs, crew practices also include activities such as running on treadmills or running stairs. In the off-season, rowers are wise to continue their aerobic training by running, bicycling, or, for those who have access to it, cross-country skiing.

Serious competitors, such as those training for the Olympics, use heart-rate monitors to give them exact readings of their aerobic capacity. Everyone else who shares the goal of preparing for an endurance event should shoot to train at 70 to 80 percent of maximum heart rate (the point just below the anaerobic threshold). You can roughly calculate this number by subtracting your age from 220. For example: A twenty-year-old's maximum heart rate is 200, so his desired training zone would be between 140 and 160 beats per minute. What's a simpler way to determine whether you're training in your desired aerobic zone? When you can't easily carry on a conversation but you are not yet out of breath.

STRENGTH TRAINING

Enormous strides have been made in physiological research during the last several decades. Coaches and oarsmen have extensive resources available to learn about strength, power, and endurance training. A number of good books and dozens of articles available through the USRowing resource library (accessible online at usrowing.org) provide detailed training regimens and charts to measure performance.

Coaches agree that weight lifting is a crucial component of performance in rowing today. At many practices, coaches and trainers incorporate circuit training, which combines weight lifting with aerobic training—a great solution for time-pressed oarsmen.

It hasn't always been this way. Years ago, oarsmen were reluctant to train with weights because they feared that bulking up would actually hamper their performance. Part of this misconception came from the notion of weight lifting as a practice wherein bodybuilders isolate certain muscles and work to make them as big and "ripped" as possible.

Then, as more knowledge became available, rowers and their

A stable core makes for a stable boat.

coaches realized that strength (not bulk for aesthetics' sake) was a good thing. Rowers benefit greatly from sport-specific strength training that emphasizes multijoint movements and core stability.

Aaron Benson, women's novice lightweight coach at MIT in Cambridge, Massachusetts, developed the weight-lifting programs for the school's entire rowing program. including men and women. In the pages ahead, you'll find some of Benson's thoughts on training and some specific exercises to try.

Resistance Training There are three types of muscular fitness: endurance. strength, and power.

Endurance—being able to exert the same force over and over for a long period of time—comes first and takes longest. Starting with lighter weights allows proper technique and decreases the risk of injury.

Strength—maximal force production—comes second, after a solid endurance base has been established. This type of lifting involves more traditional ideas of sets and repetitions.

Power—producing near-maximal force with rapid movement—is the final phase, heading into competition. Dynamic movements are emphasized, and risk of injury is greater, so it's important that proper technique be formed during the endurance phase.

Following are some useful lifts for rowers. These are fairly simple, require little equipment, and have a relatively low risk of injury. Still, a rower should always have supervision and instruction when undertaking a resistance training regimen, especially when performing more difficult lifts, such as deadlifts, leg presses, and bench presses. In all lifts, the torso should remain in a neutral position, with a natural curve to the spine.

Lunge. Stand upright and step forward. Lower down so that the knees of both front and rear legs bend to 90 degrees (the rear thigh should be vertical and the front thigh horizontal), then stand upright again and repeat with the opposite leg forward. Lunges can be done in place by bringing the front foot back or by "walking," bringing the rear foot to the front on each repetition. Keep the torso upright and do not rest hands on the thighs. Carry weight at the sides or across the back. Lunges give the most bang for the buck, working flexibility while also building muscle.

Squat. Stand upright with feet straight and slightly apart. Squat down as though sitting on a chair, extending the hips back. Align the shoulders directly above the feet, and go down as deeply as possible without losing the lumbar curve in the lower back; then stand up again. Ideally, at the bottom of the squat the thighs will be horizontal. Carry weight across the shoulders behind the head (back squat) or in front (front squat). Once you can squat at least your body weight, do a one-legged squat with weight held in the hands to provide a further challenge for the core muscles.

Power pull. This is a combination of the deadlift and the upright row. Begin at the bottom of a squat with a bar hanging in front of the shins. Stand up and pull the bar up to neck height.

Push-up. Lie on the ground, face down, with palms on the floor under the shoulders. Extend the arms and keep the body stiff to push up off the floor. Lower down and repeat. This can be made easier by resting on the knees instead of the toes, or made more challenging by placing one hand or both hands on a medicine ball.

Pull-up. Hang from a bar (overhand grip) and pull the chin up over it. A partner can assist by pressing up under the knees as you bend the legs 90 degrees.

Core Training Strong muscles in the trunk—the abdominals, obliques, and back extensors—help brace the spine with good posture, protecting it from injury and allowing effective transfer of power from the legs and hips out to the oar. The core muscles are good power generators for rowing (or for many other sports), so it is best to train them statically for endurance, to maximize power transfer from the extremities.

There are three simple exercises that will build stability in the trunk. These exercises should be done daily, if possible, and take only ten to fifteen minutes to complete. A single repetition involves holding the position for eight seconds; allow only a couple of seconds in between repetitions. Three sets are performed with fewer repetitions as the muscles become more fatigued—a set of 5, a set of 4, and a set of 3.

Curl up. Lie on the back with hands under the lower back to support the lumbar curve. Keep one leg straight and bend the other to 90 degrees (it does not matter which one). This will keep the pelvis aligned. Curl up with upper back to bring shoulders barely off the ground, keeping the lower back neutral. The head will lift off the ground, but keep the neck aligned (do not bring chin to chest).

Side-bridge. Lie on your side, place the foot of the upper leg in front of the other foot, heel to toe. Lift into side plank position, with forearm on floor (rest on the elbow). Shoulders and hips should be vertical and square to each other. To switch sides, turn shoulders and hips together (ribs locked to pelvis); place opposite arm down, and roll over. Do sets of 5, 4, 3, alternating sides within the set (i.e., left, right, left, right, etc.).

Bird-dog. Start on all fours. Stretch one leg straight out behind and bring the opposite arm straight out in front. Shoulders and hips remain square and horizontal. Back is neutral. Between repetitions, swing the leg and arm down without touching the floor and swing them right back into the next repetition.

Any time these core exercises are part of a longer workout, be sure they are the last exercise. It is not a good idea to fatigue the core before doing something else active, especially rowing or lifting. That approach begs for an injury. Furthermore, breathing hard before doing core work helps an athlete learn how to take deep breaths while still bracing the abdomen for support.

These exercises can be made more challenging by holding a complete abdominal brace—tensing the abdominals, obliques, and back extensors (all the muscles that form a natural weight belt) simultaneously.

■ The best winter activity for rowers in the north, besides working on the ergs, is cross-country skiing.

■ One of the best ways to rid the body of toxins and eliminate lactic acid (a rower's enemy!) from the muscles is through massage.

■ Be sure to avoid lifting weights that work the same body parts two days in a row.

■ When beginning a weight-lifting program, start slow and remember that soreness is common.

STRETCHING TIPS

- Stretch only when your body is warmed up.

- Never bounce while stretching.

- Stretch until muscles feel tight but stop before you feel pain.

- Hold stretches for 10 to 30 seconds.

- Don't hold your breath while stretching. Take deep, full breaths.

- Stretch as often as possible, every day if you can.

Flexibility Every sport has an ideal range of flexibility to maximize performance and minimize injury. In rowing, the athlete's shoulders should be stable, and the hips and ankles should have good range of motion.

The only rower's muscles that need to be consistently stretched are the hamstrings. Lengthening them enables a rower to pivot the torso forward from the hips so that the spine can be in a better posture. Remember, a rounded back is likely to become an injured back.

Several of the exercises from Jaryn Finch's warm-up sequence are good for enhancing flexibility. Here's another move targeted to stretch the hamstrings: Lie on your back and have a partner lift up one leg at time, straight up, until a stretch is felt (keep the back neutral and hips on the floor). Push the leg against the partner for ten seconds, then relax and let the partner push the stretch further; hold for several seconds. Do this after the muscles are warm, ideally at the end of a workout.

FEED ME

Food is fuel for athletes. An oarsman who doesn't consume enough calories soon finds himself running out of steam, whether he's in the gym or on the water.

There may be more books (not to mention newspaper and magazine articles) written about diet and nutrition than any other topic. The USRowing resource library has several dozen articles that provide detailed information on the specific nutrition needs of novice, lightweight, masters, and Olympic rowers.

For everyone, from national team competitors to recreational rowers, an excellent resource is the *Sports Nutrition Guidebook* (third edition, 2003), by Nancy Clark, with information that can help rowers determine the best nutritional plan for them.

Low-carb fads come and go, but athletes rely on carbohydrates for performance, especially wholesome, complex carbohydrates such as those found in multigrain breads or oatmeal. Athletes need to maximize glycogen (carbohydrate) stores for both training and competition.

Protein is an important part of the diet, but athletes will find that too much protein may hinder their performance, as the body digests proteins relatively slowly. Therefore, it's especially important to avoid too much protein right before a race.

In addition to eating a well-balanced diet, the best thing a rower can do to enhance her performance and keep from feeling fatigued is to drink water. Hydration is extremely important, especially on race day. Water should be drunk throughout the day leading up to a race or a practice. If an oarsman waits to hydrate until right before, during, or after a row, it may be too late. The National Athletic Trainers' Association (NATA) recommends drinking 16 to 20 ounces of fluids two hours before working out.

Food and Water Tips

■ Small, frequent meals are best to help avoid energy dips caused by low blood sugar.

■ Avoid high-fat and high-sugar snacks and meals. These can slow you down faster than catching a crab.

■ Try to get your vitamins from real food, as opposed to supplements. Protein, minerals, fiber, and energy are best utilized by the body when provided by actual calories.

■ Aim to consume five liters of water on workout days.

■ Carbo-load throughout the week before a race and for the first four hours after a race for optimum recovery.

■ Don't overeat late the night before a race. Also, try to eat a light breakfast the morning before a competition.

■ During a workout or race, you are burning what you ate and stored 24 to 48 hours earlier.

■ Experiment with diet and hydration during practice—not during a race!

Aerobic: A stage of a workout when all of the body's need for oxygen is met by what is being inhaled and what is already stored in the body. This state can continue for a long time.

Anaerobic: A stage of a workout when the body's need for oxygen is not met by what is being inhaled or by what is already stored in the body. This state cannot continue for long because it causes a painful buildup of lactic acid.

Ergometer: A rowing machine that closely approximates the actual motion of rowing, using a flywheel and a digital readout so that the rower can measure his strokes per minute and the distance covered.

Flick it in: Slang for not working hard, or coasting through a piece.

Piece: Any period of work performed in the shell—for example, a 10-minute piece, a 500-meter [546.8-yard] piece, or a 20-stroke piece.

Get warm.

"It is only following 5,000 repetitions done exactly the same way at low speed that a skill becomes automated; then the skill can be successfully transferred to a higher intensity training and performance."

—*Skillful Rowing*

6: FACE FORWARD

The Role of the Coxswain in the Crew

Wanted: Small person with a very big mouth. Ability to steer and cheer essential.

Possibly the most unusual position in all of sports belongs to the coxswain. Where else—except when riding a racehorse—is it an enormous benefit to be as small as possible? Where else—except when calling plays in a noisy football stadium—is it a major plus to have a loud voice? And where else—besides on a bike or an Indy racecar—is an ability to steer absolutely essential?

Enter the coxswain, or as rowers like to say, the "cox."

About the Cox

A coxswain is the person (male or female) who normally sits in the stern of the boat—typically a four or an eight, sometimes a pair—and steers by moving the rudder and giving instructions to the crew (using a megaphone or, more typically these days, an electronic microphone). The cox, the only member of the crew who faces forward, also sets the pace and motivates the crew, among many other duties.

NOTE: Occasionally the cox will be seen in a different position: lying down in a well in the bow of the boat. Although it is becoming a bit more common, this is still the exception to the rule.

What Makes a Good Cox?

Size Since one of the goals of every crew is to keep the boat as light as possible, when it comes to coxes, the smaller the better. Since women tend to be smaller than men, it is not unusual these days to see women "coxing" (rowers regularly use this verb) for men's teams. (USRowing Rules note that a male coxswain may compete in events for women, and a female coxswain may compete in events for men.) The smaller size preference also encourages participation from those who may not otherwise get the opportunity to be involved in the sport.

USRowing Rules state:

A coxswain in an event for men's crews shall weigh at least 120 lbs [54.5 kg].

Crews on big boats won't get far without a good cox.

A coxswain in an event for women's crews shall weigh at least 110 lbs [50 kg]. Coxswains who do not comply shall carry deadweight, such as sand or other ballast, in order to achieve the minimum weight. Any such deadweight shall be placed in the boat as close to the torso of the coxswain as possible, and it is specifically forbidden to distribute deadweight throughout the boat. Excess clothing, equipment, electronic systems, tools, or other utilitarian devices germane to competition, shall not be considered part of the coxswain's weight and shall not be included as part of any deadweight required.

Smarts A cox has to be in the know. To give effective commands during a race he needs to know his crew's strengths and weaknesses. He needs to be prepared to give feedback after practice or a race, and, perhaps

The cox is a crew's link to their coach.

most importantly, he needs to know the racecourse, and be able to navigate it well.

He also needs to be very familiar with all equipment so he can let the coach know whether adjustments need to be made and so he can make repairs in an emergency.

Confidence Despite their smaller stature, coxes must have the self-assurance to lead their crew in rigging the boat, running practice drills, and rowing a race.

KEEPING ON COURSE

Steering is something that must be learned in the boat with plenty of trial and error. Coxswains steer *figuratively*, by commanding only the port oars to row, for example, and *literally*, by adjusting the tiller, which in turn moves the rudder.

The first step, once seated in the boat, is to set your palms on the gunwale and grasp the tiller knobs using your thumb and first two fingers. Your third and fourth fingers (of each hand) should be around the gunwales so you can press against the gunwales and hold yourself in the boat.

Most coaches say: "Only steer with the rudder when the oars are in the water."

But Yasmin Farooq, the world champion cox who posts tips on her Web site Coxswaination.com, takes a more nuanced approach:

■ The best way to initiate a turn is to move the tiller at the beginning of the drive and hold it in place over several strokes.

■ Make sure the actual motion of steering involves pushing the tiller knobs, not pulling them.

■ To go to starboard, gently push the right tiller knob forward. To go to port, gently push the left tiller knob forward.

■ To make minor shifts or adjustments, try to steer on the recovery. For best results, gently nudge the tiller.

Literary Digest, **1921.** Courtesy of the National Rowing Foundation.

■ Do things gradually to maintain the balance of the shell.

Most importantly, communicate with your crew and let them know where the other boats are.

Communication A loud, clear voice is a bonus for a cox, but with today's technology (almost everyone uses microphones), diction and the ability to give clear instructions are more important. The message is what really matters.. Coxes are often the on-the-water link between the coach and the crew.

Dedication Coxes earn the respect of their crews not only by being successful on the water but by showing a willingness to train during practice and learn techniques alongside the rowers.

Essential Equipment

Besides these qualities, a good cox should be prepared with the right equipment. Today, high-tech devices that were unheard of just twenty-five years ago are now standard in every stern (or bow). No coxswain can live without his cox box (a combination amplifier/stroke meter/timer) and, in many cases, the newer voice-activated transmitter/receivers (to communicate with the coach when out of megaphone range).

Here's what USRowing has to say about the use of these devices:

A boat may be equipped with an internal loudspeaker system and electronic devices that provide statistical information about the progress of the race or performance of the crew (such as elapsed time or stroke rate). During a race, no boat shall have on board any electronic devices that are capable of sending or receiving information from any source external to the boat, regardless of whether it is actually used. The possession within the boat of any radio device is specifically prohibited.

Besides the electronics, here are some things every cox should have on his checklist:

- Megaphone
- Tools (such as screwdrivers and pliers for equipment adjustment and repair)
- Spare parts (rigger and wing nuts, lock washers, oarlock spacers, side pins)
- Pen and paper (to make notes for feedback)
- Tape recorder (for self-critiques)
- Wristwatch (waterproof)
- Water bottle
- Electrical tape (for equipment repair)
- Sunscreen
- First-aid kit

FLOATING
FIRST AID

A cox should stock his
first-aid kit with:

- Band-Aids
- Athletic tape
- Antiseptic wipes
- Adhesive bandages
- Hydrocortisone ointment
- Cold compress
- Tweezers
- Space blanket

Most coxes are not also rowers, although it is common to see a sidelined oarsman serve as cox while he is recovering from an injury. This is a great way for someone who can't row to stay involved in the sport. Even though most coxes do not row competitively, it definitely is a good idea for them to learn the mechanics of rowing so they can give tips and feedback to the crew.

Coxing is a sport in itself, and it is very competitive. Even though it's not exactly physical, there is a lot of mental preparation and understanding of rowing that goes into coxing a boat.

It's important to remember that even though the cox is not technically a rower, he is still a member of the crew and subject to the same rules as his crewmates on and off the water.

A coxswain's role is extensive: he is basically in charge of organizing and directing the crew before, during, and after a race or practice. This includes setting up and putting away equipment and doing training drills in the gym or tanks. Here are some of his duties, in order of importance:

1. Safety
2. Steering
3. Managing the crew and equipment
4. Orders (moving the boat, starting the crew)
5. Enthusiasm
6. Advice and corrections on technique

The cox leads the way.

COMMANDS

Since coxes are responsible for directing the rowers on and off the water, they will need to know the following vital cox commands (from USRowing's coxswain handout):

"Way enough": Pronounced "way-nuf"; tells rowers to stop rowing or to stop walking when they are carrying the boat.

"Hold water": Tells rowers to place their blades in the water and to hold them there until the boat comes to a stop.

"Sit ready": Tells rowers to prepare to row.

"Ready all, row": Tells rowers to start rowing.

"Let it ride": The command for rowers to keep blades out of the water after they have stopped rowing and to let the boat ride or glide.

"Up two, in two": The command for the stroke oar to raise the stroke rate two strokes per minute from the current stroke rate, and for the crew to do the same after two strokes are taken.

"Down two, in two": The command for the stroke oar to lower the stroke rate two strokes per minute from the current stroke rate, and the crew to follow after two strokes.

In addition to these standard commands, many coxswains at all levels find it effective to develop

COX TALK

What do some coxes say to motivate their crews?

- ■ "You're gods!"
- ■ "Quick!"
- ■ "Sharp!"
- ■ "Jump!"
- ■ "Hop!"
- ■ "Push . . . swing!"
- ■ "You love it!"

What do some coxes do to motivate themselves?

- ■ Listen to tapes of famous coxswains winning races.
- ■ Work out with the crew—running stairs, on the ergs, in the tanks.

Steer clear: A cox holds a crew's safety in his hands.

their own verbal shorthand to use on the water. These phrases should be rehearsed with the crew ahead of time. In her article "Five Keys to Competitive Coxing" Yasmin Farooq, the cox for the U.S. National Team Women's Eight (1989–1996) and inventor of the Yaz Cam video camera for coxswains, gives an example of abbreviating a ratio call (used when the crew is rowing at the correct stroke rate but the balance between drive and recovery is out of whack). "When I first started using it I would say, 'Slide comes down one beat, power with leg drive (or body swing) goes up one beat . . . get set . . . on this one," says Farooq. "But that took too long to say, so we changed it to, 'Ratio call . . . get set . . . on this one.'"

To Swear or Not to Swear?

Although there are ever-present bleeps over the voices of coxswains on tapes of many races, from collegiate rivalries to national championships, swearing is not encouraged. In fact, swearing at another boat in competition will get you an unsportsmanlike-conduct penalty.

It's also an excellent idea to create shorthand for things specific to the crew, such as identifying a rower's particular problem with technique and calling it his "checkpoint." Farooq goes over a specific correction with a rower before practice so that out on the water, all she has to say is, "Mary, checkpoint."

Further, many crews have a secret racing move, saved for emergency situations, that may be called up with one phrase known to all. For example, at the 1990 World Championships in Australia, Farooq's crew had the "flex." The crew knew it would be used only once and that when she called, "Flex! On this one!" they would row their very best ten of the race.

So, if you're small in size and up to the challenge, climb aboard. Because, like rowing, the only way to really learn coxing is by getting out on the water.

More Tips

- Learn the racecourse ahead of time by perusing maps or taking a preliminary trip over the course.
- Less is more: rowers tend to ignore coxes who talk nonstop.
- It's more effective to project your voice than to shout.
- A calm voice is usually the most effective.
- Critique yourself by taping practices and races and playing them back.
- If you need to diet to make weight, do so early in the season, and be sure to eat on race day.

Cox box: A device used by coxswains that gives information about the crew, including its speed, stroke rate, number of strokes, and time rowed.

Rating (or stroke rate): The number of strokes rowed per minute.

Rudder: A hinged fin mounted on the stern or beneath the hull of a shell, controlled by two cables connected to the tiller or by two wood handles called *clackers*.

Rudder cable: A cable or rope that a coxswain pulls or pushes to turn the rudder.

Rudder stem: The metal bar that extends through the deck and hull through a small hole and connects the rudder to the rudder bar.

Settle: The part of the race, per the coxswain's command, when the crew decreases the rating from the initial high stroke to a lower pace that it will maintain until the final sprint.

Tiller: A coxswain's steering bar made of wood or metal, connected to the tiller ropes, which in turn are connected to the rudder.

Toggle: A wooden or plastic handle attached to the rudder cable to provide a better grip.

Woodie: A homemade tool used to loosen and tighten wing nuts on the boat.

Behind every great crew there's a cox.

A boat with no coxswain is called "coxless" or "straight." A boat with a coxswain sitting in the bow is called "bow-coxed" while one with a cox sitting in the stern is said to be "stern-coxed."

7: CALL ME COACH

What to Do When You're in Charge of a Crew

Say "crew coach" and what image pops to mind? For anyone who has seen shells gliding along a river, it's probably the coach following his crew in his motorized launch, megaphone in hand. The launch is an essential tool for a coach (imagine him trying to keep up by *rowing* alongside his crew) and an important part of the safety equation in rowing, since it enables him to keep a watchful eye on his rowers and transport safety or repair equipment to them if necessary.

The launch is the common denominator for crew coaches. But the similarities end there.

TYPE A OR B?

There are two stereotypes for crew coaches. The first is the taciturn type. This coach is serious, dedicated, decisive, smart, and tough, and he doesn't say much. His word is law and his rowers are in awe, if not in fear, of him. This type is all but defined by Harry Parker, the legendary longtime coach of the Harvard crew (as well as many Olympic and U.S. National teams).

Then there is the boisterous type. This coach holds nothing back. He yells, he cajoles, he explains, he stomps his feet on the boat ramp, and he cheers until he loses his voice. The University of Washington's Dick Erickson is a well-known example of this kind of coach.

In reality, depending on the level of the crew and their goals, most coaches fall somewhere in the middle.

"There are all kinds of coaches," says Hart Perry, Executive Director of the National Rowing Foundation and former coach (for thirty-four years) of the prestigious Kent School crew in Connecticut. "But I think if you scream all the time people stop listening to you!"

Jaryn Finch, the JV girls coach for the Massachusetts Public High School state champs

ACCENTUATE THE POSITIVE

- Speaking in specific terms to explain what a rower should do to correct an error is much more effective than pointing out what he did wrong.

- End every practice and race on a positive note.

- Communicate to your crew that every stroke is an opportunity to improve.

- Remember, this is supposed to be fun!

Do as I say . . .

from Brookline High School, agrees that it takes all kinds. "There are many different approaches," she says. "I'm a more emotional coach. I'm vocal and try to communicate my passion for the sport. For the crew I'm coaching, it's better that way. We have a third boat—they are the girls who are trying to get in the first two boats but can't necessarily make it there. So you have to find a way to keep them committed because they don't have the drive of simply doing well to keep them here."

Coaches definitely need to find their own way to inspire new rowers to keep rowing.

"That is your most important job as a novice coach," says Allen Eubanks, head coach of the Oak Ridge Rowing Association and chairman of the USRowing Youth Committee, "to make it so kids want to continue. Because your first year, it's not about competitiveness. Eventually it is, but you have to hook them first."

Most coaches agree that instilling a love of the sport in novices is an admirable goal. But if coaches of crews at all levels had to name their very top priority, safety would definitely top the list.

COACHING TOOLS

- Launch
- Megaphone
- Notebook
- Stopwatch/stroke counter
- First-aid kit

Speak softly but carry a big megaphone.

SAFETY FIRST

"Attention to safety is the number-one thing to look for in a coach," says Glenn Merry, Executive Director of USRowing. "That is absolutely the most important thing."

Next on the list?

"You need someone who is well organized and an effective communicator," Merry says. "Then comes rowing technique and understanding of the sport."

That may sound backward—putting the actual *rowing* part last—but Merry and others with experience on the water know that safety is crucial and that even the most experienced rower won't succeed as a coach if he can't run a smooth practice and teach young rowers what he knows.

USRowing, which has an excellent three-tiered certification program for coaches, recommends that any club or school looking to hire a coach make sure he or she at least has completed Level One of the program.

TOO MUCH PAIN, NO GAIN

Pain is a major factor in rowing. In fact, for many rowers it's a badge of honor, and the unspoken rule among rowers is not to complain about pain. An important job for a coach is to find the balance between encouraging and pushing the crew and knowing when a rower might be hurt and needs to stop.

So How Does a Crew Coach Coach?

Once again, safety is stressed above all. USRowing's Safety Bulletin (available at USRowing.org) is full of detailed instructions for dealing with minor and major emergencies, such as heat exhaustion, heat stroke, and hypothermia. Coaches should also check the Web site for a Pre-Practice Safety Checklist, which includes a list of supplies and steps your crew should take before hitting the water.

Here's what he doesn't do: coach during the rowing of a race. USRowing Rules forbid a coach to communicate with his crew once a competition is underway. But practice days are a different matter.

Since coaches often have crews for only a limited time (for example, the MIT crew is restricted by collegiate rules to a two-hour maximum), efficiency is key. A good coach has an instinct for how hard to work his crew; most coaches find it effective to stagger workouts through the week, alternating challenging workouts with lighter ones.

TIP: Never schedule a tough practice right before a race.

A coach should also establish a balance between training exercises in the gym and time on the water. He also needs to factor in time for feedback, questions and, of course, boat maintenance.

One of the best things about coaching a crew, according to Glenn Merry, is that once the boats launch, you have your athletes' undivided

The coach decides who sits where.

A Coach Is ...

A teacher

A counselor

A diplomat

A fundraiser

A motivator

A doctor (or at least a paramedic)

According to Glen Merry, Executive Director of USRowing, a great coach exhibits the following qualities, in order of importance:

1. Attention to safety.

2. Organization and effective communication.

3. Knowledge of rowing technique and understanding of the sport.

attention. "Once they're on the water, they're strapped in," he says. "They have to pay attention. If they don't follow everyone else, someone is going to get an oar in the back or throw off the entire crew. This is one of the only sports where, once we get started, kids can't really goof off. The distractions are limited."

Coaches also have the undivided attention of their crews when it comes time to seat boats—possibly a coach's most important function. "Seating" means that after evaluating an oarsman's strengths and weaknesses, the coach determines who takes which place in the boat. Some

$ $ $

Today, coaches for most scholastic programs and all collegiate and national team programs are paid for their work. This wasn't always the case. In the late 1800s and even the early 1900s, "pro" coaching was frowned upon as something that tainted the sport. These days a coach's knowledge and experience— not to mention the time he is required to spend with his crew—are more highly valued. No coach, even in the most prestigious program, is going to get rich, but the pay scale is improving.

For a coach in search of a position—or for parents or alumni wanting to find a coach for a program—a good place to

Princeton Coach Duncan Spaeth, 1925. Courtesy of the National Rowing Foundation.

start is the Row2k.com Web site. The monthly magazine *The Rowing News* also regularly prints job listings. And it pays to talk to people at other rowing programs. The rowing community nationwide is extremely tightknit. If you're looking for a coach or looking to become one, someone at a club or another school can probably help.

of the criteria for seating a boat are predetermined—usually, lighter rowers are positioned in the bow, while stronger rowers often take the middle. But determinations are also made based on the rowers' performance and personality. Since the seating of a boat can make or break a crew during a race, it is a great coach who masters this talent.

Shhhh! Coaches are forbidden to communicate with their crews in any way once a race has started.

One way a coach determines who will row in which boat (and in which position), with the goal of setting up the fastest possible boat, is through *seat racing*. The coach sets up a race between two boats, following them in his trusty launch. After their race, he swaps one rower from each crew to the opposite boat. Then they race again.

The theory is that he can determine who is the faster rower by changing only one pair in the second race. But even when the coach does his best to keep the conditions consistent, this is not an exact science. And many rowers dislike seat racing because, in order for it to work, they can't know who is being tested.

In sum, a coach needs to have plenty of knowledge about sports medicine, psychology, and rowing equipment and technique. He has to be dedicated and never expect to get rich. But he gets to work outside and work with kids or adults who will take away a love of rowing, something they'll keep for the rest of their lives.

As Hart Perry said of his time at Kent, "Coaching high school was so rewarding because you get to see kids change dramatically in four years. You look back at kids who you thought would never take to rowing and they ended up being great."

A View from the Launch

As a coach, the best moment you can experience is when you're working with novice rowers, sharing with them your passion for the sport, and they take that first stroke, when everyone in the boat is all together and the boat moves smoothly across the water. The look on their faces is incredible! You know then that your passion has become theirs, and they will now spend all their time trying to achieve that moment over and over again. . . .

There are several top-quality coaches working in the youth rowing ranks. The sport is as pure at the youth level as it has been for centuries. Youth programs across the country introduce rowing to kids who are in middle and high school. The athlete in these kids is still unknown at this age so it's important for coaches to build solid programs. It's crucial for youth recruitment and development to be the same as it is at the college and the elite levels of rowing, if not tougher. The youth boat speed may be a bit slower but the competition is just as real. . . .

Coaching at the youth level gives you the experience to build on. My coaching style comes from a mixture of my previous sports involvement, the Army, and the way I was trained to row. But mostly my knowledge base comes from what I have been able to gather through books and those great coaches who have let me share their launches.

Even though rowing is the oldest sport in the country, it is still new to the Southeast. The Southeast is producing five to ten new programs a year! This is partly a function of all the people who migrated south from the Northeast and brought rowing with them. At our club, it was the adults from MIT and Dartmouth who first wanted to row, because they had rowed in college. Soon after the adults began to row, area kids became interested and approached them about learning to row, and Oak Ridge Juniors were born.

I feel that some of the enormous growth is partially due to Title IX and the rising numbers of women in the sport, which has resulted in greater exposure and, consequently, greater knowledge and awareness of rowing. There are incredible opportunities for girls these days, in the form of scholarships, since the NCAA governs women's collegiate rowing. I look forward to the day that the SEC recognizes rowing and the region just explodes with strong, solid youth and college programs.

The whole point is to have fun. I try to teach kids that first. Of course, it's okay to win, too. Winning is fun! But that shouldn't be the only goal. Anyone who gets into rowing for the winning or the money will be very disappointed because you're not going to win all the time and you're not going to make much money. So my goal is to get them to love the sport for their own reasons. When they do that, and when they learn to pull on that oar together, there's nothing better. Today, coaches for most scholastic programs and all collegiate and national team programs are paid for their work. This wasn't always the case. In the late 1800s and even the early 1900s, "pro" coaching was frowned upon as something that tainted the sport. These days a coach's knowledge and experience—not to mention the time he is required to spend with his crew—are more highly valued. No coach, even in the most prestigious program, is going to get rich, but the pay scale is improving.

For a coach in search of a position—or for parents or alumni wanting to find a coach for a program—a good place to start is the Row2k.com Web site. The monthly magazine *The Rowing News* also regularly prints job listings. And it pays to talk to people at other rowing programs. The rowing community nationwide is extremely tightknit. If you're looking for a coach or looking to become one, someone at a club or another school can probably help.

By Allen Eubanks, Head Coach, Oak Ridge Rowing Association; Southeast Representative and Chairman, USRowing Youth Committee; Director, Southeast Junior Rowing Development Camp

COMING TO TERMS

Practice—not race day—is the time for critiques.

Heat exhaustion: Signs are throbbing headache, nausea, cool but sweaty skin, chills, and weak pulse.

Heat stroke: Can be life-threatening. Victim may exhibit behavior changes; become unconsciousness; have hot, flushed, but not sweaty skin and rapid pulse.

Hypothermia: After being exposed to cold temperatures, cold water, ice, or snow, victim becomes disoriented and feels cold, turns bluish, shivers, and begins to feel numb, apathetic, and lethargic.

Launch: The coach's small, motorized boat he uses to follow his crew.

Logbook: A sign-in/sign-out book every coach should put in the boathouse and insist his crews use to monitor who is on and off the water.

PFD: Personal flotation device or life jacket. Coaches should carry these on the launch, making sure to have one for every rower on the water.

Seat racing: A method to compare individual rowers' performances, whereby the coach orders two (or more) crews to race, usually for two or three minutes. When they stop, two rowers switch boats and the crews race again.

In the early days of rowing, coaches would often follow their crews on a bicycle along a riverside path and shout instructions to them on the water. Coaches' launches forever changed how crews were coached.

8: THE RACE IS ON

All about Crew Competition

Some rowers take up the oar and step into a shell purely for exercise or for fun. But most oarsmen and their teammates put in countless hours of practice on the water, in the tanks, and in the gym with one end result in mind: the race.

According to USRowing Rules:

Race: The rowing of the course in a competitive manner by one or more crews, the results of which are used as part of the process to determine the winner and order of placement in an event.

Regatta: A combination of different events sponsored by the same local organizing committee as a single unit.

RACE CATEGORIES

Traditionally, there are two kinds of rowing competitions or regattas—head races and sprint races—as well as championship events, among them some hotly contested titles.

HEAD RACES

Head races, or head starts, which normally take place in the fall, are the longer races, usually consisting of a course between three and six kilometers long. They take their name from old English races in which the

Spring means sprints.

winner was declared "Head" of the river. The largest and most famous in the United States is Boston's Head of the Charles Regatta, where every year, since October 1965, rowers of all ages, abilities, and affiliations have come to compete. Today, more than seven thousand athletes from around the world, including Olympians and elite college crews, row in this prestigious race.

With seven thousand competitors, it would be impossible to start all the boats in a category at once, or even in two or three heats, so the Head of the Charles, like other head races, staggers its competitors, who are judged according to their times. Head races can be challenging: not only are they longer than sprints, but the courses vary from race to race, and crews must be aware of current strength, turns, and wind direction. Boston and Cambridge, the towns that line the Charles course, are exciting places to be during this spectacular event, where boats move nonstop down the river for two full days.

SPRINTS

As the name implies, sprints are shorter, faster races, two thousand meters (approximately 1¼ miles) or less. High school sprints are usually fifteen hundred meters but can be as short as five hundred meters. Sprints always have boats (usually three to six) starting together and rowing to an exciting finish. Events at championship regattas, such as the Federation Internationale des Sociétés d'Aviron (FISA) World Championships and the Olympic Games, have six buoyed lanes in a straight course, as most sprints do. But, occasionally, seven or eight boats will line up to start.

HOLD 'EM

All sprints begin with boats aligned together in the lanes they have been assigned. Volunteers or officials in each lane hold the stern of each boat steady from their idling launches, known as *stake boats*, while an official, called the *aligner*, ensures that each boat is even with the others and squarely facing the course.

Large regattas, such as the annual San Diego Crew Classic, organize crews to compete in flights, where the winner is final, or a series of heats and semifinals whose winners move on to the finals.

CHAMPIONSHIPS

USRowing sponsors national championship regattas every year for all Elite, Senior, Intermediate, Junior, and Junior B events. Other highly anticipated events include the Masters National Championships and the Youth National Championships.

Every year since 1894, the Intercollegiate Rowing Association (IRA) has sponsored a collegiate national regatta, whose winner is widely considered to be the men's national champion.

Since 1997, collegiate women have competed as part of the NCAA, the governing body for most college sports. Since the NCAA does not hold a lightweight championship race, the IRA hosts a women's lightweight event.

Other important championships in the world of collegiate rowing are the Aramark Central

Rested and ready.

Region Championships and the Pac-10 championships, which include men's and women's crews, among them California, Stanford, Oregon State, and Washington.

Arguably, most prestigious of all are the Eastern Sprints, events hosted by the Eastern Association of Rowing Colleges (EARC) for men and the Eastern Association of Women's Rowing Colleges (EAWRC) for women.

**All eyes
on the water.**

The winners of these are declared Ivy League Champions, a designation some rowers say is the ultimate.

SECOND CHANCE

In many races, including the Olympics, World Championships, and NCAA Championships, rowers who have already lost a heat get another chance to qualify for the semifinals in a second-chance race known as a Repechage. This often makes for exciting competition and allows a crew that may have not had the best conditions to show its real stuff.

Race times vary considerably, depending on the course and weather conditions. Tailwinds will improve times while headwinds and crosswinds will hamper them.

RACE RULES AND STRATEGY

Most crews start out fast, even out a bit, then sprint to the finish. But according to John McArthur, author of *High Performance Rowing*, the most economical way to cover any race distance is to maintain an even pace from start to finish. This, McArthur says, is the approach of the majority of top-class, international crews. But this is easier said than done. It is very tempting to sprint from the start or to sprint at the finish, and, in fact, many crews have won races this way. But when planning a race strategy, crews are wise to spend practice time well ahead of race day to determine the boat's cruising pace, the maximum speed rowers can row without accumulating too much lactic acid in their bloodstreams. This way, a realistic cruising goal can be set and met.

All those hours of practice lead up to one thing: race day.

Despite this "steady wins the race" philosophy, and as important (obviously!) as the finish is, most crews put a great deal of emphasis on a strong start. One reason is that in the first twenty strokes of a race, a boat can gain or lose up to three-fourths of a length. This is the only place in a race where a crew can gain or lose so much in such a short period of time.

Coaches should run as many start drills as possible in the weeks before a race. (See USRowing.com for sample start drills.)

Here are some tips for a strong start:

- Before the start, rowers should have their blades squared in the water and ready to go. Up to that point, the oars may float freely, but when the starting command is near, they should be squared and buried.
- During the first few strokes of a race (especially the very first stroke), bury the blades slightly deeper than normal for extra resistance.
- Carry the blades a bit higher than usual on the recovery.
- Focus on quick and complete feathering.
- Start the race with shorter strokes and work up to longer ones.

Every race has its own specific rules and designations, depending on the particular host or sponsoring organization. Here are a few regulations from USRowing Rules that oarsmen may want to know:

Few sports have as great a disparity between time spent during practice and time spent in an actual game or race. An elite rower may practice as many as 475 hours in a given year but race only about two hours.

Rowing Near the Course While Race in Progress

Whenever a race is approaching, a non-competing crew rowing at or near the perimeter of the course shall stop rowing, come to a complete rest, and make sure that it does not interfere with the race, either by obstructing the path of the competing crews or accompanying launches, or by causing a wash.

Approaching the Start; Warm-up on the Course

No crew shall enter the starting area until the previous race has cleared and unless explicitly permitted to do so by the Starter. Except where required by the posted traffic pattern, a crew shall not practice on the course itself during the time when racing is taking place without permission of the Starter.

After a crew has been given permission to practice on the course, it shall do so only in its assigned lane. If it is necessary to cross other lanes to reach its assigned lane, a crew shall yield to any other crew practicing in its own lane.

Reporting to the Start

Each crew is responsible for being attached to its starting station and ready to race two minutes before the scheduled time of the race, whether or not announcements have been made by the Starter. If racing is delayed, crews shall be responsible for being within voice range of the Starter and in a position to respond to instructions.

The Starter shall, whenever practicable, announce the time remaining to the start of the race at five, four, three, and two minutes to the start.

A crew that is not attached to its starting station at least two minutes before the scheduled time of the race may be assessed a warning by the Starter. A crew that is not attached to its starting station by the scheduled time of the race may be excluded by the Starter. If racing is delayed, the

Starter may announce a new racing time, which shall have the same effect as the original scheduled time for purposes of this rule.

Polling

After the Judge at Start signals that alignment has been achieved, the Starter shall poll each crew to see if it is ready to race. Polling shall consist of calling out the name of the crew. If a crew is not ready, either during polling or thereafter, the bowperson shall signal by raising his or her hand conspicuously in the air.

If alignment is lost during the polling of the crews, or if a crew previously polled signals that it is not ready, the Starter may suspend the polling process and resume when the previous condition is restored. If there is a significant delay, the Starter may repeat the entire polling procedure.

The mighty shell sits at the ready.

Starting Commands

After the crews have been polled, the Starter shall start the race by: (1) calling out "Attention!," (2) raising a red flag overhead, preferably using two hands, and (3) after a distinct and variable pause, calling out "Go!"

The command "Go!" shall be accompanied by a quick downward motion of the red flag to one side.

If, after the red flag has been raised, the Starter believes for any reason that the start should not occur, he or she shall call out "As You Were!" and gently lower the red flag directly in front of him or her. The Starter then shall repeat the starting commands in their entirety, but may dispense with re-polling the crews.

Crews may leave the starting line when the Starter's red flag begins to move.

Unless the Starter believes that a crew is engaging in intentional delaying tactics or other unsportsmanlike conduct, he or she shall recognize a crew signaling that it is not ready, except where the "countdown start" is used. If the race is started while a crew is validly signaling before the start that it is not ready, that crew shall remain at the start. A crew that rows out of the starting area (100 meters) [about 110 yards] waives any right to protest on the grounds that the start was not fair.

Any official in the starting area may stop the race if he or she observes a crew signaling that it is not ready.

Each crew is allowed one false start; two means disqualification. If within the first hundred meters there is legitimate equipment breakage (e.g., an oar snaps in two), the race will be stopped and restarted with repaired equipment.

"Quick Start"

If weather or other conditions prevent use of the normal starting procedure without inordinate delay, the Starter may dispense with the polling procedure. The Starter first shall announce to the crews that a "quick start" will be used. When all crews appear to be properly pointed and ready to race, the Starter shall immediately give the starting commands. The Starter shall nevertheless recognize a crew that signals before the start that it is not ready, regardless of when such signal occurs.

"Countdown Start"

If it appears to the Starter that conditions prevent use of either the normal starting procedures or a "quick start" without inordinate delay, he or she may resort to a "countdown start." The Starter first shall announce to the crews that a "countdown start" will be used. At an appropriate juncture, and without further polling the crews, the Starter shall count down in regular cadence: "five—four—three—two—one," and give the starting commands in normal cadence. It is the sole responsibility of the crews to point their boats while the countdown is in progress.

The Starter may disregard any crew signaling that it is not ready under this procedure, regardless of when such signal is given.

The Body of the Race

A Crew's Water: Each crew shall be assigned a lane, which shall constitute that crew's own water for the duration of the race. A crew that rows in its own water is entitled to protection by the Referee. A crew that leaves its own water does so at its own risk and peril.

Steering: Each crew is responsible for its own steering. The Referee will not render assistance to crews merely to steer a better course, even if a crew leaves its own water, and will instruct a crew to alter its course only to prevent interference, or otherwise ensure safety, or to ensure fairness to other crews.

Instruction to Avoid Unsafe or Unfair Conditions: If a crew is steering toward a previously known or identified obstacle or installation and is in reasonable danger of collision, the Referee shall alert the crew by calling out the name of the crew and raising a white flag vertically, and then call

Coach Allen Eubanks pumps up his crew from Oak Ridge, Tennessee, before the 2006 Southeast Regional Youth Championships in Tampa, Florida.

out "Obstacle!" If collision is imminent, the Referee shall order the crew to stop. That crew then may correct its course and continue with the race, but shall not be entitled to any consideration, such as a re-row or advancement in the progression system, as a result of such occurrence.

If a crew is steering towards a previously unknown or unidentified obstacle or installation obstructing its assigned lane, and is in reasonable danger of collision, the Referee shall alert the crew by calling out the name of the crew and raising a white flag vertically, call out "Obstacle!," and instruct the crew to alter its course. If collision is imminent, the Referee shall order the crew to stop, after which it may correct its course and continue with the race. If the opportunity of a crew to win or advance is affected by such occurrence, the Referee may take appropriate action to restore that opportunity.

If a crew is rowing outside its assigned lane and is thereby in a position to gain an unfair advantage, either by shortening its course or by receiving the benefit of more favorable environmental conditions such as wind or current, the Referee shall instruct the crew to return to its lane. If the crew does not comply with such instruction, in the absence of any specific mandated penalties the Referee may impose any one of the penalties described in "Types of Penalties."

Nothing in this rule shall preclude a local organizing committee from adopting regatta rules, which mandate that a specific penalty be uniformly applied for one or more lane violations. Any such penalty must be described in detail in the application to USRowing for registration and must be publicized in writing and distributed to every competing team.

The Finish

The Order of Finish; Dead Heats: A crew has finished the race when its bow or any part of its hull touches the plane of the finish line. It shall be considered a dead heat if two or more crews finish the race simultaneously, or if the judges, after having used all best efforts and available resources, are unable to determine the order of finish with reasonable certainty.

If a dead heat occurs in a finals race, and if a proper order of finish is necessary to determine which crews are entitled to medals or awards, the Referee shall order the crews involved in the dead heat to re-row after a rest interval. If a crew refuses to re-row, the Referee shall award the higher place being contested to the other crew, and he or she may exempt it from re-rowing the course. If a re-row is not practical, the Referee may order that duplicate medals be awarded.

Physiologists claim that rowing a 2,000-meter race (1.25 miles) takes the same physical toll as playing two back-to-back basketball games.

If a dead heat occurs in a race other than a finals race, and if a proper order of finish would be necessary to determine which crews advance in the progression system, the Referee shall, wherever possible, allow all crews involved in the dead heat to advance. If such action is not possible, the Referee shall order the crews to re-row, after allowing for a rest interval, and after having taken into account the scheduled time of the next race in the event. If a crew refuses to re-row, the Referee shall award the higher place being contested to the other crew, and he or she may exempt it from re-rowing the course.

Head races: Mostly held in the fall, these races feature a running start, where crews cross the starting line while moving at predetermined intervals. Winners are the crews with the lowest time.

Power 10: When the coxswain calls for the crew's most intense ten strokes during a race.

Repechage: The second-chance race that ensures that everyone has two chances to advance from preliminary races, since there is no seeding in the heats.

Sprints: Races on courses of 2,000 meters or less, where boats line up and start simultaneously and sprint to the finish. Almost always held in spring and summer.

Starting area: The first 100 meters of the course, as well as the adjoining water at the perimeter of the course.

Strokes per minute (SPM): The unit by which rowers measure their speed, literally the number of strokes the crew completes in a minute's time. The stroke rate is high at the start (maybe 45 or even 50 for an eight, 38 to 42 for a single scull). The crew settles into the body of the race and drops the rate back—38–40 for an eight, 32–36 for a single. Most crews sprint to the finish, taking the rate up once again.

Unsportsmanlike conduct: Includes but is not limited to: failure to heed the instructions of race officials; use of obscene language or gestures; delaying a race without just cause; intentional or flagrant disregard of principles of safety and fairness; or abusive behavior toward any official, team member, or spectator.

9: Make It Official

Crew Referees

Every competition, from the humblest local regatta to the grand Head of the Charles, needs a referee (or referees) to keep things organized and to make sure the outcome is fair.

Rowing officials are part of a special breed, and their duties, which primarily take place on race day, are specific and steeped in tradition.

What Does It Take to Be a Ref?

According to USRowing Rules:

It is the primary duty of every race official to provide for the safety of competitors and officials.

It is the duty of all race officials to ensure that all crews have a fair and equal opportunity of winning or placing. Where a crew has been affected by unfair advantage or disadvantage, whether due to another crew or outside circumstances, it is the responsibility of race officials to restore fair racing conditions.

Probably the most important thing a rowing ref needs is enthusiasm. Also, since officials are volunteers, every referee needs a strong commitment to the sport.

Although past rowing experience and familiarity with the sport are definite pluses, USRowing does not require referees to be former rowers. Local clubs and scholastic teams around the country are finding that nonrowing parents of rowers and coaches, as well as former coxswains, often turn out to be excellent refs.

Learning rowing terminology is, however, nonnegotiable. Basic organizational skills and the ability to project your voice and give clear, crisp commands are essential as well. Also, since safety is the first priority at any regatta, a referee needs to be confident that he can provide for the safety of fifty or more people on the water.

The finish line is finally in sight.

THE REF STUFF

Official Uniform

- Shirt
- Patch
- Hat

Official Equipment (All Refs)

- Megaphone
- Flags

Official Equipment (Starters)

- Updated schedule
- Effective starter's flag
- Noisemaker, to stop races
- Radio or telephone
- Public address system (a lapel or stand-up microphone)
- Lectern or stand with digital clock (and a large clock for the rowers)

BECOMING A REFEREE

Regardless of past rowing experience, anyone—including those who have never rowed!—who meets USRowing requirements can become an assistant referee. Then, if interested, an assistant can work toward becoming a full-fledged referee. The first step is to contact USRowing and be directed to the regional referee coordinator in your geographic region.

To become a licensed assistant referee, a candidate must:

- Be a USRowing member.
- Attend a referee clinic covering the Rules of Rowing.
- Be at least twenty-one years old or be a college senior and a participant in an intercollegiate rowing program.
- Have normal sight, hearing, and mobility, sufficient to sustain routine activities.
- Show proof of the ability to swim two hundred yards.
- Observe the following positions to understand their roles and responsibilities: marshal, chief referee, starter, referee at start, referee, and dockmaster.
- Pass the assistant referee exam, a written test covering the Rules of Rowing, after meeting the above requirements.

SEVEN REASONS TO BECOME A REFEREE

- You love the sport of rowing.

- You want to learn more about rowing and to teach others.

- You would like to give back to your rowing community.

- You want to connect with people who share your love for rowing.

- You are a parent, family member, or friend of a rower, and want to become more involved in that person's rowing activities.

- You are a collegiate rower in your last competitive season and you are looking for a way to stay involved in the sport after graduation.

- You are tired of racing backward and would like to see the sport from a different seat!

To become a fully licensed referee, an assistant referee must:

■ Be a USRowing member.

■ Attend a clinic every year.

■ Work a minimum of four regattas per year.

■ Be exposed to the following positions for at least the number of times indicated and complete an evaluation form each time: marshal (2), referee at start (5), starter (5), chief referee (5), referee (10), and control commission (2).

■ Work for a minimum of fourteen regattas before sitting for the referee exam—at least twelve sprint races and at least two head races.

■ Work two national standard regattas.

■ Work at a minimum of four different race courses. It is recommended that one of these be out of the assistant referee's home region.

■ Submit a referee data form to the referee vice-chair every year. This form is mailed to all referees by the committee in September.

■ Pass the referee exam after meeting the above requirements, between twenty-four and forty-eight months after passing the assistant referee exam. The exam has both practical and written parts and is conducted by a three-person panel.

NOTE: It usually takes from two to four years to complete the requirements to become a referee.

To maintain a license once earned, a referee must:

■ Be a USRowing member.

■ Attend a clinic every year.

■ Work a minimum of four regattas per year.

The ref is ever-watchful on the water.

The USRowing Referee Commission supervises training and continuing education of officials throughout the country. The commission, which meets two or three times a year, and by email and conference call, works to ensure the highest standards of safety, fairness, and ethical conduct in the rowing community and the fair and consistent application of the Rules of Rowing. It also acts as an arbiter of appeals to protest rulings, conducted by on-site juries, and determines the validity of licenses of referees, the assignment of chief referees to national regattas, and the nomination of referees for international regattas.

TIPS FOR REFS

■ Buy a powerful, sturdy megaphone.

■ If you've never rowed, be sure to at least go out in a shell. Take a shot at coxing a boat for a club crew to get the feel of the water.

■ Remember, referees are not paid and must provide for their own equipment and travel.

■ Anyone considering becoming a ref may want to start by volunteering to drive a referee's launch.

RACE DAY

Before every regatta, the USRowing Referee Commission appoints a Chief Referee, who has a long list of duties to perform. These begin with selecting additional officials who are needed to run a race. Here are the specifics, according to USRowing Rules:

2-103 Duties of the Chief Referee

(a) The Chief Referee:

(1) shall assign the functions of all other race officials at the regatta;

(2) shall be President of the Jury;

(3) may act individually as a race official as described in Rule 2-104 ("Officials");

(4) shall verify the existence of safety requirements at the regatta site, and shall execute an appropriate document reporting his or her findings and send it to USRowing headquarters;

(5) shall perform such other functions as are assigned to him or her under these Rules.

(b) If these Rules call for a decision by the Chief Referee, the Chief Referee may refer such matter to the Jury for resolution.

(c) Assignment or appointment of race officials made by the Chief Referee, including members of the Jury, shall be subject to review and revision by the USRowing Referee Commission but shall not otherwise be subject to challenge, review or protest before the Jury or another race official.

2-104 Officials

(a) For each race at a regatta, the Chief Referee shall cause to be assigned officials to perform the following functions:

(1) Referee: The Referee shall have general supervision of the race and shall follow the progress of the race from start to finish. All other officials for a particular race shall be subject to the control of the Referee except where duties are specifically dictated to them under these Rules. If more than one official follows the progress of a race, the official who begins the race following behind the lanes closest to the Judges' stand shall be the primary Referee, and all others shall be secondary Referees.

Unless otherwise indicated, reference in these rules to the "Referee" shall include both the primary and secondary Referees.

(2) Starter: The Starter shall administer the starting procedures and shall be responsible for their fairness. The Starter may be assisted by a deputy.

(3) Judge at Start: The Judge at Start shall supervise the process of bringing the crews into alignment with the plane of the starting line, shall decide when a crew has left the starting line before the proper commands, and may otherwise assist the Starter. The Judge at Start may be assisted by an Aligner provided by the local organizing committee.

US ROWING WANTS YOU!

In 2006, there were just over six hundred licensed rowing officials in America. With the growth of the sport and the fact that so many schools and clubs want to compete on the same weekends, the rowing community desperately needs more referees. The first step to earning your stripes is to call USRowing and to be put in touch with a local representative.

(4) Chief Judge: The Chief Judge shall supervise the judges at the finish line and, along with the judges, shall inspect photographic records of finishes to determine the proper order. If there is disagreement, the finding of the Chief Judge shall prevail over an individual judge.

(5) Judges: Under the supervision and control of the Chief Judge, the judges shall determine and

record the order of finish, when necessary inspect photographic records of finishes, determine the proper placement of crews, and compute the appropriate time margins.

(b) All persons acting as Referee (primary or secondary), Starter, Judge at Start, or Chief Judge at any registered regatta shall have a Referee or Assistant Referee license.

2-105 The Jury

(a) Before the regatta, the Chief Referee shall appoint a Jury.

(b) The Jury shall normally be comprised of five members, including the Chief Referee as President.

A different number may be designated by the Chief Referee, provided that there is an odd number of members, and that there are no less than three members.

Jury members shall have a valid Referee or Assistant Referee license.

(c) The Jury shall:

(1) hear and decide all protests arising out of competition;

(2) decide matters referred to it by the Chief Referee.

(d) The decision of the Jury made within its jurisdiction shall supersede any decision of an individual race official.

(e) When the Jury is hearing and deciding a protest as authorized under subsection (c)(1) above, no official shall serve as a member if the issue to be decided involves a decision made by that official, or if that official must give testimony as a witness. The Chief Referee shall designate an alternate member to serve instead.

> "The best situation for a referee is when after a race, the crews didn't even know he was there."—HART PERRY

Red flag!
The race is on!

FLAGS

Among the many terms and procedures an aspiring ref must learn,
perhaps the most important are the
nonverbal commands, communi-
cated with flags. Although other colors (usually orange) are sometimes
used to mark the finish, official referee flags are either red or white.

Red flags, also called *starting flags*, are used by the starter to signal
the beginning of the race. When the starter raises his flag above his head,
then thrusts it downward, the race begins. Red flags are also used to warn
crews that drift out of their lanes and to signify a race under protest.

NOTE: Red starting flags may also feature a white crisscross
design for better visibility.

White flags are mostly used for all-clear signals such as when the
boats are aligned at the start of a race and ready to go. The referee on the
water would also raise a white flag to signal to the rowers and the Chief
Referee at the finish that the race is officially over. The Chief Referee then
raises his white flag to return the signal and accept the finish time. Also,
if a crew is in danger of colliding with a known obstacle, the referee will
raise the white flag directly overhead and give the command, "Obstacle!"

NATIONAL STANDARD REGATTAS

Officials learn the ropes and fill an important role at many different
rowing competitions, but none are as important as National Standard
Regattas. As defined by USRowing:

. . . *National Standard Regattas are events that have been singled out by the*

Referee Commission as models for the entire rowing community for excellent management. They are meant to be teaching/learning venues for referees and substantially meet the requirements of a Class A course. This designation is an honor and establishes the regatta has followed the highest standards. Referees must officiate at one of these events on a regular basis to keep their licenses current. Organizers of smaller regattas are encouraged to visit one of these regattas as a model.

NATIONAL STANDARD REGATTAS

The Referee Commission has established the following events as National Standard Regattas (if USRowing-registered):

USRowing Youth National Championship Regatta

USRowing National Championship Regatta

USRowing Masters National Championship Regatta

Middle Atlantic:

Virginia State Championships

Stotesbury Cup

EAWRC Women's Sprints

Dad Vail Regatta

IRA Championships

Independence Day Regatta

Head of the Occoquan

Head of the Ohio

Head of the Schuylkill

Midwest

Midwest Championships

Midwest Junior Championships

Indianapolis Collegiate Invitational

Head of the Rock

Head of the Des Moines

Head of the Elk

New England

New England Rowing Championships

ECAC Championships

EARC Men's Sprints

Northwest

USRowing NW Junior Regional Championships

USRowing NW Masters Regional Championships

Green Lake Spring Regatta

Green Lake Summer Regatta

Green Lake Frostbite Regatta

NCRC Championships

Head of the Lake

Southeast

USRowing SE Regional Championships

SE District Youth Championships

Southern Intercollegiate Rowing Association (SIRA) Championships

South Central Sprints (NCAA) (Aramark)

John Hunter Regatta

Florida Intercollegiate Rowing Association Regatta (FIRA)

Head of the Chattahoochee

Head of the South

Head of the Tennessee

Southwest

San Diego Crew Classic

USRowing SW Regional Junior Championships

Pac-10 Championships

WIRA Championships

COMING TO TERMS

ACCORDING TO USROWING:

Race official: *The Chief Referee, members of the Jury, or any other person who serves at a regatta in one of the capacities described in USRowing Rule 2-104 ("Officials"), and who possesses a valid USRowing Referee license.*

OTHER TERMS EVERY REF SHOULD KNOW:

Aligner: The official who brings the crews even to the plane of the start, either talking directly to them or through headsets to the stake boat holders.

Disqualification: A serious offense that causes the crew to be excluded not only from the race but from any subsequent races at the same regatta. The crew's actions are reported to the Referee Commission for examination. Individuals may also be disqualified. Examples: flagrant and intentional violations of fairness and safety at a regatta, or abusive language or action taken toward other competitors or officials on or off the water.

Exclusion: When conduct of a crew is deemed egregious enough to warrant its removal from a race, either because of a foul, a serious violation of the Rules of Rowing, or the accumulation of a second warning.

Primary referee: Also called the *secondary* or *suppliant referee*, this is an informal designation of the referee covering the lower-numbered lanes in a race that has two separate referee launches. Sometimes this second referee withdraws after the first five hundred meters of the race is safely completed. In international competitions, there is only one referee launch per race.

Protest: A crew's request of an official to rectify a wrong done to them in the course of the competition by restoring their chance at a better placement in a race. The protestor states the infringement and the remedy sought. Any protest for race incidents must be lodged on the water at the end of the race with the official who has followed the race; that official may uphold or deny it there. If the protestor is not happy with that official's decision on the water, he or she may then ask that the jury be convened to hear the protest more formally on land. In the latter case, the race results are unofficial until the protest has been resolved.

Referee at the Start: The official who determines by watching both the start flag and the bows at the line if any crews jump the start. (At large regattas, he often has the benefit of a split-screen TV to monitor the crews.) He is the sole determiner of a false start, and stops the race when this occurs. At smaller regattas, the Aligner and Referee at the Start are often the same person.

Reprimand: A verbal sanction imposed on a crew by an official for a minor violation of rules or procedures at a regatta so that the crew may rectify it at once without incurring a more serious penalty. A reprimand imposes no handicap on a crew. Repeated instances of the same or similar violations may incur a stronger penalty. Examples: wrong bow number on the shell, lack of uniformity in dress in a shell.

Warning: A serious imposition on the crew for a violation of traffic, safety, rules, or good sportsmanship. A warning is recorded and accompanies a crew for the duration of the race, or can be carried into a subsequent race if the warning was imposed outside of a race situation. A second warning for any offense excludes the crew from its race. Examples of warnings: false start, violation of traffic pattern en route to a race, or after a race (in which case, the penalty is carried with the crew into its next heat or final).

Sacramento Shuffle: A launch placement, developed by Bob Scurria at the PCRC in Sacramento, California, that places referees every five hundred meters along the course as monitors. After a race passes him by, each monitoring referee moves back toward the start by five hundred meters until eventually he becomes the referee going down the course. In this way, only one referee is needed to take a race down the course, and wakes are minimized by officials in the race and by those returning to the start for the next race. Also, safety is enhanced by having competent rescue/safety/officiating boats in reserve all along the racecourse, who can join in the race at any point where they are needed. This kind of progression works especially well at championship events with competent crews when there are sufficient numbers of referees and launches to accomplish its goals.

Afterword

This is an exciting time for athletes who are interested in getting involved in rowing and for those who are seeking to start crews at their schools or in their towns. The opportunities have never been greater.

One of the most inspiring things about crew is that it welcomes many athletes, young and old, who have never participated in sports at all. A high school senior who never tried out for the football team can excel on a crew and enjoy the benefits of being part of a team. A college freshman who may have not considered playing a sport may be recruited by a novice coach, who thinks the student looks like a rower, and go on to compete nationally. A college graduate who moves to a traditional rowing town, such as Philadelphia or Boston, or a new rowing town such as Tampa, will find it easy to join a club and get out on the water.

The first step to joining a club or a scholastic or collegiate team is to get in touch with USRowing and find a local contact. If your school or area does not sponsor a crew, USRowing can put you in touch with other nearby schools or clubs that may be willing to share resources, such as their boathouse and equipment, while your crew gets started. It also helps to ask around and find enthusiastic rowing alumni in your area to lend a hand. USRowing can also help a new crew find a coach and train interested crew fans to become referees.

Equipment, though still expensive, is more widely available these days thanks to the rise in the number of shell manufacturers in the last decade. More manufacturers also means they want your business, so a fledgling club might be able to negotiate a payment plan for new equipment. Also, more crews means more secondhand equipment is available, some of it in tip-top shape. Elite university crews often rotate out their equipment after just three years.

Spend five minutes on the ramp of a boathouse on a sunny spring morning and you will learn what all rowers know: rowing gets into your blood.

Appendix: Basic Rigging

For both the beginning coach and the expert, the only purpose of rigging is to allow the rower to apply power in the most efficient manner. Rigging is often perceived as a mysterious blend of Zen and voodoo! Nothing is further from the truth. Rigging is making simple mechanical adjustments to the parts of the oar and the shell in order to make the rower comfortable and effective. Following the instructions and using the recommended settings in the charts provided here will provide you with all that is necessary. The hardest part is being able to detect which mistakes on the water might be related to the boat's rigging. Developing an eye comes with experience. Unfortunately, we can't give you that in this appendix, but we can get you off to a good start.

Tighten up: Be sure to rig your boat right.

Rigging Adjustments

Whether rigging a new boat or checking the adjustments on an old boat, the procedure is the same. Be prepared to record the measurements in your coaching notebook.

Measure: Spread and inboard settings, height, pitch, and footstretcher settings.

By Mike Vespoli, USRowing Coaching Education, Level I. A copy of this article along with illustrations, is also available from the resource library on the US Rowing website (usrowing.org). A copy of the article may also be obtained by calling 800-314-4ROW.

Spread: The distance from the center of the boat to the center of the pin.

For sculling boats, spread is the distance from the center of the pin to the center of the opposite pin.

This distance will determine the length of the arc in the water. Shorter spread means a sharper, longer arc and "heavier" work; longer spread means a flatter, shorter arc and "lighter" work.

Spread also determines the comfortable length of the inboard measurement. As a rule of thumb:

For sweep boats:
Inboard = spread (+) (30–31) cm [12–12¼ in.].

For sculling boats:
Port inboard (+) starboard inboard = spread + (18–22) cm [7.1–8¾ in.] of overlap.

Of course, there is an important relationship between the inboard and outboard portions of the oar length. This relationship will define leverage, which also can change the work from "heavy" to "light."

Fortunately, as coaches we are spared the necessity of making these calculations all the time. The most economical lengths of spread, as well as length of oars (inboard + outboard length) have been calculated and put in tabular form for each category of boat as shown on the next page.

The most common mistake made by beginning coaches where rigging is concerned is that they copy measurements from the tables of elite-level crews, failing to realize that those crews are bigger, fitter, and more skillful than their own. The result is a much heavier rig than is

Suggested Measurements for Sculling Boats, Club Level (1x, 2x, or 4x)

	SPREAD (in. / cm)	INBOARD (in. / cm)	SCULL LENGTH (in. / cm)	OVERLAP (in. / cm)
MEN	62¼–63 / 158–160	34.7 / 88–88	117 / 298	7.1–8¾ / 18–22
WOMEN	62¼–63 / 158–160	34¾–35⅛ / 88–89	117 / 298	7.1–8¾ / 18–22

Suggested Measurements for Sweep Boats, Club Level

	SPREAD (in. / cm)	INBOARD (in. / cm)	DAR LENGTH (in. / cm)	OVERLAP (in. / cm)
MEN:				
Pair without	34–34¼ / 86–87	45¾–46 /116–117	152 / 383	12–12¼ / 30–31
Pair with	34¼–34¾ / 87–88	45¾–46½ / 116–118	152 / 383	12–12¼ / 30–31
Four without	33–33½ / 84–85	45–45¼ / 114–115	152 / 383	12–12¼ / 30–31
Four with	33½–34 / 85–86	45¼–45¾ / 115–116	152 / 383	12–12¼ / 30–31
Eight	32¾–33 / 83–84	44½–45¼ / 113–114	152 / 383	12–12¼ / 30–31
WOMEN:				
Pair without	34–34¼ / 86–87	45¾–46 / 116–117	150 / 378	12–12¼ / 30–31
Four without	33–33½ / 84–85	45–45¼ / 114–115	150 / 378	12–12¼ / 30–31
Four with	33½–34 / 85–86	45¼–45¾ / 115–116	150 / 378	12–12¼ / 30–31
Eight	32¾–33 / 83–84	44½–45¼ / 113–114	150 / 378	12–12¼ / 30–31

appropriate. We advise that for club and college purposes, the coach use the table provided here.

With the same length of oars, the longer spread and longer inboard measurements from this table will mean a shorter arc and lighter work. Observe the drive of your crew at racing cadence. Analyze whether the drive looks too slow and sluggish—the rigging looks too heavy, or the drive is too fast and without resistance—the rigging is too light.

HEIGHT

The height of the oarlock from the lowest point of the seat is very important in achieving an efficient and powerful application of power. Correct height will be demonstrated by nearly horizontal arm level during the drive, and adequate space for a comfortable release and clearance at the finish.

Begin by setting the heights to some predetermined measurement, say 6½ inches (16.5 cm) for the starboard rigger and 6 inches (15 cm) for the port rigger on a single, or 6¾ inches (17 cm) for men's heavyweight eight.

To check the comfort of these predetermined heights, sit your crew in the shell at the finish position with the blades squared and buried. Look at the height of the hands relative to the rib cage. If the handle meets the body at the second or third rib from the bottom, then the oarlock height is suitable to begin with. To accommodate the crossover of the hands and handles in sculling boats, it is necessary to provide clearance by raising the starboard oarlock around ¾ inch (1.5 cm) more than the port oarlock.

Properly adjusted oarlocks translate into maximum power.

PITCH

Stern pitch is the sternward angle of a blade between absolute vertical and how it is positioned in the middle of the drive. Following are the most frequently used measurements:

Sweep: 5 to 7 degrees (experienced rowers, 4 to 6 degrees)

Sculling: 4 to 6 degrees

Lateral pitch, or outboard pitch, is the angle of the pin away from the gunnel, usually 1 to 1.5 degrees. It makes the stern pitch decrease as the oar moves to the finish in the drive. This keeps the blade buried in the water to the very end of the stroke.

Too little pitch makes a horizontal drive and clean finish very difficult. A rower who has water running more than a foot up the shaft of the drive may be experiencing the effects of too little pitch; conversely, a rower pushing a big mound of white water may have too much. Before changing the pitch, a coach should measure the current angles. Note these measurements in your coaching log, along with any observations about the blade's path through the water, with your recorded measurements.

Pitch can be measured directly against the face of the oarlock, if you are sure that your oars have zero degrees of pitch built in. Many coaches attempt to measure the pitch in an oar blade by putting the oar in the oarlock and simulating the blade's position in the water relative to the boat. This is very difficult to do accurately and, therefore, is not recommended. There are too many variables considering the height of the handle, the position of the blade in the oarlock, and the lateral level of the boat, which can give quite misleading measurements.

Most modern boats have riggers with adjustable pitch, or oarlocks with a pitch adjustment, that make tilting the face of the lock in the desired direction quite simple. To measure the amount of change, a pitchmeter is necessary. A pitchmeter is a simple measuring device with a movable pointer, a movable level attached to the pointer wand, and a degree scale. It would be advisable for coaches to obtain a pitchmeter, and practice pitch adjustment under the supervision of a mentor coach.

SETTING THE TRACKS AND FOOTSTRETCHERS

The relationship between the tracks and the footstretchers is important. Boats with adjustable tracks enable coaches to achieve the proper finish angle of the oar to the boat. It is important that the finish angles be the same for all rowers in the boat in order to achieve precise finishing timing—that is, all rowers getting out of the water at the same time and relative position. Without this finish timing, poor balance is likely to occur.

In sculling, the relationship of tracks and footstretchers is tied more closely to the spread and the inboard setting of the oars than in sweep rowing. Let us assume that both the proper spread for the given oar length and the sculler's ability have been set. Have the sculler sit in the boat without putting his or her feet into the shoes. Next, the sculler should find the finish position where the handles of the sculls (hands) are about 8 inches (20 cm) apart and in front of the body.

If the hands are able to pass the body to the sides, it means that the footstretchers should be moved forward toward the stern of the boat. If, at the finish, the hands are less than six to eight inches apart, the footstretchers should be moved backward toward the bow of the boat.

A lot of sweep boats are equipped with very long tracks, up to $31^{1}/_{2}$ inches (80 cm), which can cause confusion. For our natural style of rowing, with not too much compression, the most economical and practical length of the tracks is $28^{1}/_{2}$ to 30 inches (72 to 76 cm) maximum. A common mistake that coaches can make is to place the tracks too far forward (too much through the pin). In this case, the rowers slide too far, their body positions become much too upright, and they suffer from extreme overcompression at the entry. The coach, in this case, wonders why his or her crew has such trouble trying to achieve the natural style when they looked so compressed at the entry position.

Here are a few practical tips that should help avoid major problems and should also provide desirable and correct angles at the finish:

■ Use shorter tracks of $28^{1}/_{2}$ to $29^{1}/_{4}$ inches (72 to 74 cm) from the front stop to the back stop.

■ Set the back stops, as measured from the pin line, for women at $22^{1}/_{2}$ to $23^{5}/_{8}$ inches (57 to 60 cm), and for men at $25^{1}/_{2}$ to $26^{1}/_{2}$ inches (65 to 67 cm); for very tall men, $26^{3}/_{4}$ inches (68 cm).

Once you have set your tracks for the entire crew to the prescribed measurement, put the crew in the shell and let them sit with their legs fully extended. Make sure the wheels of the seat come within at least a centimeter of the bow stops on the tracks, and then set the footstretchers. Setting the rowers to the back stops ensures equal finish angles. Next, depending on the oar angle at the catch, each rower must use as much slide travel and compression as is required. A short rower may have to use all the track available, whereas a taller one with long arms may only use three-fourths of the track. The different amount of track used is not important if a wide variety of rower heights and body types exist within the crew, because the crucial entry and exit angles of the oar are the same.

Tools

To measure rigging and make adjustments, a coach will need some basic equipment.

- A 5-foot (1.5-m)-long long straightedge to measure the height of the rigger from the seat. A piece of aluminum angle or square tube is best if it is straight and won't warp.
- A tape measure with both metric and U.S. standard markings. You will need this to measure the length of the oar, the position of the button, the spread of the rowing pin, and the height of the oarlock.
- A pitchmeter. There are commercially available devices for measuring the pitch in the oarlock and on the blade. Check with your Regional Technical Coordinator or USRowing for information on where to obtain a pitchmeter.
- Assorted screwdrivers (both slotted and Phillips) and wrenches (box and open-ended, as well as crescent types).
- A roll of plastic tape. This is useful for marking spread adjustments, to note position as well as to determine whether any slippage occurs. It can also be used for quick, temporary pitch adjustment.

The oars have it.

Unless there are gross errors in rigging, most rowers can adapt at least temporarily. And before coaches and rowers explain away poor technique by blaming the rigging, try submitting a different rower in the same seat. If that rower experiences the same technical problems, then the rigging should be checked and adjusted as needed.

Sharing boats within a program is a common phenomenon. Ideally, similarly sized crews will share the same boat so that rigging changes do not have to be made. However, when crews of different sizes must use the same boat, the most important change to be made is in the height. Without changing the oarlock height, the only way to get the smaller crew in a position to put the blade in the water is by using seat pads to raise them up, thereby lowering the rigger. This will place the crew higher in an already big boat, and you can expect some balance problems to result.

Another situation arises when only one set of blades is available for use in both fours and eights or singles and doubles. To eliminate the need for rebuttoning the oar before every row, set the spreads in the respective boats to compensate. You will compromise the inboard – spread + 30-cm (12-inch) formula slightly, but it will save valuable time for rowing.

TIPS:

The day before competition:

- Clean and oil the shell.
- Check and double-check all moving parts.
  On race day:
- Bring spare replacement parts and extra stretchers.
- Make changes in rigging only if absolutely necessary. If it ain't broke, don't fix it.

COMING TO TERMS

RIGGER PARTS/TERMS

Backstay: The metal brace that attaches to the top of the pin from the side of the shell. On some shells, it can be used to adjust the sternward pitch of the oarlock.

Face of the oarlock: The surface of the oarlock against which the oar shaft presses during the pull-through.

Flat rigging: In sculling, both oarlocks are set at level heights if technique calls for rowing one hand behind the other. If the left-over-right technique is used, the starboard locks are raised ½ to 1 inch (1.25 to 2.5 cm).

German rigging: Also called *bucket rigging*, this setup finds two starboard or port riggers are in consecutive order rather than alternating.

Lateral pitch: The angle of the pin away from the center of the shell, also called *outward pitch*. Lateral pitch is designed to combine with sternward pitch so that the pitch of the blade increases at the catch and decreases at the finish. Lateral pitch is usually built into the sill or pin and, in some cases, is adjustable. Zero to 2 degrees of lateral pitch is recommended for all boats.

Load: Also called *gearing*, load refers to the relationship between the length of the oar, the outboard length, and the spread. Load = [outboard − 8 inches (20 cm)] ÷ spread. An overall range for eights is 2.94 to 3.09, the smaller number being the easier load.

Oarlock: The plastic or metal device, often U-shaped, mounted on the rigger, that swivels and holds the oar in place.

Note: The depth to which a loaded shell is submerged affects the height of the oarlock, which must be adjusted to suit the physique of the rowers, the skill of the crew, and water conditions. Power transmission is most efficient when the oarlock is set low enough to give minimum clearance for the release of the blade. Setting the oarlocks too low will cause sloppy finishes, so beginners are usually rigged higher than elite rowers.

Oarlock gate: Also called the *keeper*, the oarlock gate is the arm that locks the oar into the oarlock.

Oarlock height: The distance from the lowest point of the seat to the middle of the bottom of the oarlock.

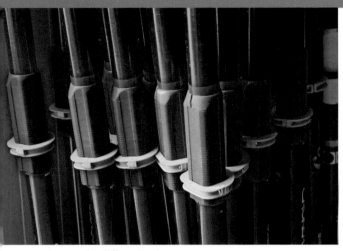

An oar of a different color.

Pin:	The vertical metal shaft around which the oarlock swivels.
Pitch:	The angle between the blade (on the pull-through) and a line perpendicular to the water's surface.
Pitchmeter:	A device used to measure pitch.
Rigger:	The triangular-shaped metal arm extending from the side of the boat that supports the oarlock and oar. Some riggers are fixed in the distance from the boat, while others are adjustable. The rigger is held to the boat by "rigger bolts" and "rigger nuts."
Shim:	An angled metal or wooden piece placed next to the side of the boat where the rigger is attached. This is used to adjust the height of the riggers.
Sill:	The platform made by the intersection of the rigger arms that support the oarlock.
Spacer:	Also called *washers*, spacers are plastic, doughnut-shaped pieces that fit around the pin and allow the oarlock height to be raised or lowered.
Sternward pitch:	The angle of the blade away from perpendicular during the pull-through of the stroke. Sternward pitch gives the blade a more even, horizontal path through the water by counteracting the blade's natural tendency to dive from the rower's hands pulling across the top of the oar. Pitch comes from several sources: the oarlock, the tiltable pin, or an oar that has pitch built in. Sweep blades are usually tilted toward the stern between 6 and 8 degrees, while sculling blades are tilted between 4 and 6 degrees. A blade diving (going too deep) on the pull-through may be underpitched, and one washing out (only partially buried) may be overpitched.

BIBLIOGRAPHY

The Amateurs (David Halberstam, Fawcett Books, 1985)

The Book of Rowing (D. C. Churbuck, Overlook Press, 1999)

Essential Sculling (Daniel J. Boyne, Globe Pequot Press, 2000)

High-Performance Rowing (John McArthur, Crowood Press, UK, 1997)

The Red Rose Crew: A True Story of Women, Winning, and the Water (Daniel J. Boyne, Globe Pequot Press, 2000)

The Shell Game (Stephen Kiesling, Nordic Knight Press, 1981)

A Short History of American Rowing (Thomas Mendenhall, Charles River Press, 1981)

Skillful Rowing (McNeely/Royle, Meyer & Meyer Sport, UK, 2002)

Sports Nutrition Guidebook (Nancy Clark, Human Kinetics Publishers, 2003)

The Strength and Conditioning Journal (periodical)

Stretching: 20th Anniversary Revised Edition (Bob Anderson, Shelter Publications, 2000)

Supertraining (Mel Siff, Supertraining Institute, 6th edition 2003)

Ultimate Back Fitness and Performance (Stuart McGill, Wabuno Publishers, 2004)

Resources

USRowing
2 Wall Street
Princeton, NJ 08540
800-314-4ROW (4769)
609-751-0700
Usrowing.org

*USRowing, the governing body
for rowing in the United States,
provides excellent resources to its
members, including coach's training,
insurance, and local rowing
contacts. The extensive resource
library offered to members includes
everything from tips on training
and how to transport equipment
to how to start a new club.*

National Rowing Foundation
Executive Director: W. Hart Perry
67 Mystic Road
North Stonington, CT 06359
860-535-0634
Natrowing.org

*The National Rowing Foundation
raises funds to support the
United States National Rowing
Team and manages the Rowing
Hall of Fame.*

Additional Web Sites

Backfitpro.com
Boathouserow.org
Coxswaination.com
Eatright.org
Mysticseaport.org
Row2K.com
Rowinghistory.net

Rowing Manufacturers

Alden Ocean Shells
383 Main Street (Route 1A)
Rowley, MA 01969
800-477-1507 (U.S. and Canada)
09-1-978-948-7692 (International)
rowalden.com

Concept2
105 Industrial Park Drive
Morrisville, VT 05661
800-245-5676
concept2.com

Dirigo USA
588 Elm Street
Biddeford, ME 04005
207-283-3026dirigousa.com

Durham Boat Company
220 Newmarket Road (Route 108)
Durham, NH 03824
603-659-7575
durhamboat.com

Empacher
Bootswerft Empacher GmbH
Rockenauer Str. 7
69412 Eberbach, Germany
06271-8000-0
empacher.com

Hudson Boat Works
Racing boats
1930 Mallard Road
London, Ontario N6H5M1
519-473-6558
hudsonboatworks.com

Maas Rowing Shells
1319 Canal Boulevard
Richmond, CA 94804
510-232-6164
maasboats.com

Nielsen-Kellerman
Waterproof Electronics
21 Creek Circle
Boothwyn, PA 19061
610-447-1555
nkhome.com

Peinert Boatworks
46 Marion Road (Route 6)
Mattapoisett, MA 02739
508-758-3020
Sculling.com

Pocock Racing Shells
615 80th Street SW
Everett, WA 98203
888-POCOCK1 (888-762-6251)
425-438-9048
Pocock.com

Resolute Racing Shells
77 Broadcommon Road
Bristol, RI 02809
401-253-7384
Resoluteracing.com

Theimann Equipment
1434 Calle Grande
Fullerton, CA 92835
619-454-8299
thiemannequipment.com

Vespoli
385 Clinton Ave.
New Haven, CT 06513
203-773-0311
Vespoli.com

WinTech Racing
345 Wilson Avenue
Norwalk, CT 06854
203-866-RACE (7223)
Wintechracing.com

INDEX

METRIC EQUIVALENTS
[to the nearest mm, 0.1cm, or 0.01m]

INCHES	MM	CM	INCHES	MM	CM	INCHES	MM	CM
1/8	3	0.3	9	229	22.9	30	762	76.2
1/4	6	0.6	10	254	25.4	31	787	78.7
3/8	10	1.0	11	279	27.9	32	813	81.3
1/2	13	1.3	12	305	30.5	33	838	83.8
5/8	16	1.6	13	330	33.0	34	864	86.4
3/4	19	1.9	14	356	35.6	35	889	88.9
7/8	22	2.2	15	381	38.1	36	914	91.4
1	25	2.5	16	406	40.6	37	940	94.0
1 1/4	32	3.2	17	432	43.2	38	965	96.5
1 1/2	38	3.8	18	457	45.7	39	991	99.1
1 3/4	44	4.4	19	483	48.3	40	1016	101.6
2	51	5.1	20	508	50.8	41	1041	104.1
2 1/2	64	6.4	21	533	53.3	42	1067	106.7
3	76	7.6	22	559	55.9	43	1092	109.2
3 1/2	89	8.9	23	584	58.4	44	1118	111.8
4	102	10.2	24	610	61.0	45	1143	114.3
4 1/2	114	11.4	25	635	63.5	46	1168	116.8
5	127	12.7	26	660	66.0	47	1194	119.4
6	152	15.2	27	686	68.6	48	1219	121.9
7	178	17.8	28	711	71.1	49	1245	124.5
8	203	20.3	29	737	73.7	50	1270	127.0

CONVERSION FACTORS

1 mm	=	0.039 inch
1 m	=	3.28 feet
1 m²	=	10.8 square feet
1 inch	=	25.4 mm
1 foot	=	304.8 mm
1 square foot	=	0.09 m²
mm	=	millimeter
cm	=	centimeter
m	=	meter
m²	=	square meter